THE WICK OF MEMORY

THE WICK OF MEMORY

New and Selected Poems 1970–2000

DAVE SMITH

WITHDRAWN

Louisiana State University Press   Baton Rouge

MM

09   08   07   06   05   04   03   02   01
5   4   3   2

Designer: Michele Myatt Quinn
Typeface: Bembo
Typesetter: Crane Composition, Inc.
Printer and binder: Thomson-Shore, Inc.

Library of Congress Cataloging-in-Publication Data:
Smith, Dave, 1942–
  The wick of memory : new and selected poems, 1974–2000 / [Dave Smith].
  p.   cm.
  ISBN 0-8071-2548-2 (alk. paper)—ISBN 0-8071-2549-0 (pbk.: alk. paper)
  I. Title
PS3569.M5173 W5 2000
811'.54—dc21

99-089440

The author is grateful to the National Endowment for the Arts, the John S. Guggenheim
Foundation, the Lyndhurst Foundation, and the Rockefeller/Bellagio Center for grants that
made many of these poems possible, and to the editors of the following, in which some of the
new poems herein first appeared (often in different versions or under different titles):
*The Black Warrior Review, College English, The Connecticut Review, Contemporary American
Poetry: A Bread Loaf Anthology* (New England University Press), *Five Points,
The New Yorker, The North American Review, The Oxford American, Poems for a Small Planet*
(New England University Press), *Poetry, The Sewanee Theological Review, The Southern Review,
The Virginia Quarterly Review, The Yale Review.*
  "Descending," originally published in *Fate's Kite* (LSU Press, 1996), appeared in *The 1997
Pushcart Prize XXI* (Pushcart Press, 1997).

Poems herein have been selected from: *The Fisherman's Whore* (Ohio University Press, 1974),
Cumberland Station (University of Illinois Press, 1977), *Goshawk, Antelope* (University of
Illinois Press, 1979), *Dream Flights* (University of Illinois Press, 1981), *Homage to Edgar Allan
Poe* (Louisiana State University Press, 1981), *In the House of the Judge* (Harper & Row, 1983),
Gray Soldiers (Stuart Wright, 1984), *The Roundhouse Voices* (Harper and Row, 1985), *Cuba
Night* (William Morrow, 1990), *Fate's Kite* (Louisiana State University Press, 1996).

The paper in this book meets the guidelines for permanence and durability of the Committee
on Production Guidelines for Book Longevity of the Council on Library Resources. ∞

To
Dee, Jeddie, Lael, Mary Catherine

Il ricordo è lucignolo. . . .

—EUGENIO MONTALE

As a small boy at the edge of the millpond I saw Shadrach not as one who had fled darkness, but as one who had searched for light refracted within a flashing moment of remembered childhood. As Shadrach's old clouded eyes gazed at the millpond with its plunging and calling children, his face was suffused with an immeasurable calm and sweetness, and I sensed that he had recaptured perhaps the one pure, untroubled moment in his life. "Shad, did you go swimming here too?" I said.

—WILLIAM STYRON, *A Tidewater Morning*

CONTENTS

From *Cuba Night* (1990)

THE WICK OF MEMORY

NEW POEMS

The Wick of Memory

THE HISTORY OF THE QUEEN CITY HOTEL

When the children ask where we came from,
I start here, with a tale of the South.

Nights, maybe our fists and cheeks bloodied
on each other, we'd pass the brick walks
where the people who had things lived,
and lay down and try to dream.
The blue hydrangeas, moon-creamed,
kept their houses in beauty. They watched us.

There, we knew, if we lived
it would be years of rooms lined
with newspaper to stay warm, smoke rancid,
staring at rain-smears on the ceiling

like a map where those before us went.
Until *they* stuck, faces
in the mud, in snow-swept streets.
Running, what blessed thing
had anyone changed?

That's how you come to a new place, you slip off,
clutching the letter that lies how better
everything is, your body aching in rooms
of the dark fouled with cousins, strangers.

★

A young woman was bent, sobbing, they gaffed her
with their fists, their uniforms glinted
under streetlights, under stars.
As I passed she reached for me,
a kind of muse I see now.

I knew I would fight them for her,

sister of trash, mother of garbage—
what they called our kind,
their words becoming my fury.

How odd to feel kinned to a stranger known only
as suffering, that thin thing in the eyes.

"Let's go," the man said after
that thunked sound of our fists on them.

He might have been my brother, just older
by a week or a year, a dark foreigner.
"You call me Uncle," he said.
A black canvas coat. Soft drawl.

He's long dead, I suppose, who slipped me
into the shadows of the Queen City Hotel.
A bottle clinked on him, too loud.
The night made me feel underwater.

I could see the moon-faces inside, just boys
like me, fire-haulers, gandies for trains,
white plates steaming
with beans, meat, and fresh bread.

I thought: I will eat meat on that china.
My head was drunk with the possibility.

★

When my dead Uncle flipped into the coop
that looped string with fishhooked corn,
we waited—Lord, it seemed a lifetime—for nibbles.
And nothing. Nothing. Then shazzam,
it was all wings flapping, blizzard
of feathers, ghosts boiling down,
and the chicken, Oh Jesus,

4

Uncle cried, please make it stop.
So I lifted the rock and did that, too.

And I stopped breathing like a shrieking chicken.
And soon we spoke like men on pine paths
as if they were carpets
in one of those rich houses.

And I saw, with that Uncle, I could go anywhere.
Useless brass locks, useless cops.

★

My Uncle's fire held a river, a sweet red flow.
We sang and lied about the shadows running,
that dead one said, like men with hope.
"Or at least some fresh chicken!"

I promised I would always remember
the stars floating in our bitter coffee.

This was before the Hotel burned,
before I got hurt so bad by the Depression,
before love that made you took my body
like a snake that swells you up.

On that night I drank my first whiskey.
I ran. I felt freed.

PULLING A PIG'S TAIL

The feel of it was hairy and coarse
like new rope in Johnson's store,
and I'd never touched any part
of a pig until that day
my father took me to farm ground
where he grew up, the woods
a kind of moving stillness, green
hanging all over. I felt I was
underwater and should be
swimming for my life, not walking
up and down bean rows until we
found pigs huddled. The farmer,
my uncle Bern, said one was mine
if I could catch him. A little one
looked easy, my size, but
wary, uncertain about many things,
the way he darted all ways
at once. I chased him while foul mud
covered me, the farmers laughing
until they cried, scooting out
to head us one way and another, all
wanting to see if I could catch
what my father had caught, and his
father, like something our kind
alone kept and venerated. I called
but that pig didn't listen, then
tired, or scared, I don't know,
it slowed and I took a grip, I pulled,
both of us grunting in pig-shit
deep as fear. Why didn't he bite?
I heard them yell the tail is yours,
it's straight! I had him, but I saw
no end to what I now held, so let go,
and dreamed. My father smoked, they said
what's life like by the ocean?

It made me think of my teacher who
yanked my hair when I kicked
the girl who said we all talked funny.
I wanted to tell my father
a pig's tail burns your hand when you
can't let go, and I wanted to go
where we lived now, the waters
spread out like a clean, fresh world.
I knew I would sleep by him,
my smell a new shadow in his clothes.

BOY WITH RINGWORM

In spatter of spring shade and sun,
I spread my grandfather's death
on his picnic table, his keys, notes
on cars he owned, travels he made,
repair kits for everything, an aerial
map of the Chesapeake Bay. Its
smell unfurls, clean, new, medicinal
as a boy's head that floats before me
out of tidal ditches we paddled. We
are almost visible in the boats, each
faint line like a skull's scar revealed.
There water kept its secret holes
you might step into, the long-hidden
feel of things that comes back when
I lean to hear the hull move, but no
rhyme or reason, as my grandfather
said, his slide rule working the table
steady as an oysterman. Things come,
things go. A finch's feather drifts
past, a man's cap overboard, too.
This map memorized the year a boy's
head got socked with sickness. None
understood, or knew why it was him.
Winter brought it, or some evil thing
boys know. By April the first gusts of
southern winds saw him nearly cured.
We fingered his sprouting gold hair
to see what joined under the blue
skin, barely. We saw worm tracks
intricate as ways through the swamp
we'd take until we drowned or rose
into lives not even priests might guess.
Why, now, is his life one I squirm
to remember, his sad gray festering
we had to touch when doctors said

stay away from your friend. We can't.
Why not us, our noses snotted,
clothes stiff in water's salt blessing,
pockets filled with fiddler crabs we'd
claim from the swamp's oozy holes,
doors, we'd boast, to the lost center
of happy men? Does any map show
rain-sting and wasp-song, how many
deaths we climbed out of with luck
we had to come to days like this?
My head whispers each place I see
in words, lush colors seasoning
to change as if wind swirls, shakes
loose red-winged blackbirds hung on
slant sawgrass like angels. I hear us,
the raucous crows, shout. Stars arrive,
settle, glare down. Flood tide twists in,
slow, certain to ferry off floaters, but
one's knee-deep in muck, and won't
give up the just-caught abundance
of fiddlers, afraid to scream, and not to,
the way he'll feel with that daughter,
just years ahead, his first child
coiled in the doctor's hands, gold hair
rings like a half-eaten mallard adrift
where the marsh rats run, they too
matted with birth's slippery dirt, no
hope he won't hear the heart man say
hours later, it's rotten luck, face
beard-scruffed, lifting as if to pray
to sea gods we'd invented once, chants
slammed at moon, and sun, and wind.
But we got him out, didn't we? Mud's
squish and suck wanted him in earth,
a star on his skull like lamp's blue fire
we rubbed until it must have hurt,
flecks, gobs sticking to us, our thin

voices knifing through fear, down
darkness of ditch where we dug hard
paddling home, not knowing why
anyone thrived or didn't, the joke
drinking and lying and memory
start telling when a boy stands up
with sickness and hurt nothing cures.
What makers failed to tell us, lost
in swamps of struggle, we lived
as tales each life makes for love.
How loud, then, we sang, who seemed
vomited out of the shallows furred
by bugs that bit us, swarming, as we
ghosts wormed our way home under
faces reading news in windows.
They heard our cries and knew us
as we would know this map's colors,
unimagined sloughs, black borders,
what crawled, slept, or bled: the life
they kept waiting for us, its parts
inexplicable, worn out, saved, boxed
in rooms whose smell makes a small path
you can't use, even understand, ever,
like a heavy keyring and a plastic skull,
mysterious tools, edges, pencils,
gizmos in some drawer meant for you.

MIGHTY JOE TURNER

Why can't I still hear love's hurt words spiraling
from his mouth, riding levels of black air laid
down on my teenage body like a wind's whisk
on pine needles? Once I felt *everything's* touch.
What was magnolia's warning, the dry velvet

of suburbs I couldn't escape, the yak of my parents?
I plugged into him. Hours I lay reading the dead's
poems teachers called ageless, gods, goddesses
strange to me as Dad's whistly Benny Goodman
until, once, dreaming Celia's new breasts, I flipped

the dial exactly where it had to be. His voice spilled
over the window's lip like summer heat that drove
crickets to rub themselves wild, it boomed, bowed,
moaned, rolled into me, wired to homemade
earphones big enough I caught each sigh, each sob.

Against my walls the sleep of my parents snored,
but my flesh crawled! The moon pooled on my belly
and Joe thumped for that woman, his big tunes
hung on midnight air like my father's suits
shrouded in closets gray and tranquil as his years.

But why do I see my father's face, not Turner's
tapping nightmares of desire, its silver gleam
night after night, waiting for me to grow, leave
dreams of Celia, the blue moon rising between
her legs, fingers starred with want? I hear him

sing mornings night tangled, and wake my soul
with tunes I can't name, not one. And Celia,
that gray shape the moon skinned in the grass,
was she only what Turner made with his mouth?
Sometimes when night air spindles right it's easy

to feel things start in black bean rows, Turner turn
as moon slips its cloud-skirt, and a motherly voice
sings in the window. We all hear it. My father rises.
Anything can happen. The dead roll from blue
dials like dreams I can't turn off, not yet, not ever.

Basement Waltz

Probably the Platters, first music
        to beckon inside, pushing my legs,
arms, snaking spinal cord—who
        knows what beat up and down, the tap
my foot took by itself working along
        until all of me trembles the way
a man starving will shove his face
        flush in desire, and gag. And she,
tulip-slender, has time left her
        now dumping the day's debris, cat
twining her sweet ankles? Does she,
        too, howl, mindless, star flare in her
eyes, lost in some memory of pain?
        I want to lift all the hours piled
like stones and walk us back
        into a black basement room, splash
in light laid down the stairs, a path
        no one has seen yet. I want rooms
we bruised ourselves in, breath, sweat,
        sliding floorboards until the dance
got too fast and we flew apart—as if we
        tried to stomp some seeping darkness
before it climbed over us. Slowed,
        then, arm in arm, we waltzed. Where,
just when I closed to kiss her, went
        hope's word Platters were singing? It
might help me to say how in my head
        she slumps helplessly, my arms
don't know what to do with her,
        I have to wait, coil against the gusts
of breath filling my ear with a word: it
        dips, an evening bat, swoops, goes,
cold as the air on a mother's cheek
        after you see what flesh is, and see
you will have to lean down, now, you

will have to kiss what's in the silk box.
But I think if I could only sing
        what that last loving word was,
the beat might come back from that hole,
        and we who wait start to sway, as
we were when all we knew was holding on.

A LANGUAGE

I'm trying to remember the mornings, scent
in my nose, her hair luffing out of my dream,
the cotton shift with her breasts slung perfectly
hidden, though the word, in truth, is *gracefully*.
That shape she lay in, a plain uncapped S, feet,
hands, knees naked and cold, the coldness over
all of her, and my hand sliding her smooth skin,
up the thigh like the secret country of the gods,
and the soft down that surprises, as Berryman
wrote in *Sonnets to Chris*. I read them to her.
She pursed lips, a little shocked, not knowing
poems hungered so, me not yet a poet. "Go on."
My hand moving, cold, roosters on her shift.

★

I like to think of you alone with me, then
your fingers that I love, relentless, playing,
and into my head gather cold's words, cold's stars,
the smell of your sleep, places, hours we lay bound
like shoestrings knotted, your vest aside, drumming
rain, lips bruised, you laughing at the bad joke
of days I called to say I've stopped loving you.
My speech slow, plain, I'm a man whose language is
a shovel, heavy and sharp-edged, who stands out
under the moon near your hedge, and digs. Softly.
Sometimes at your window my dark face gleams, chokes
words you'd fear, and hides them under the diced grass.
I mean to take advantage when you listen, as you always do.

NIGHT PLEASURES

Poquoson, Virginia

Where I come from land lies flat as paper.
        Pine, spruce, holly like dark words
left from a woods. Creeks coil, curve,
           enigmatic as women. To know the depths
you must dream. In the mountains
        for college I walked up and could see
barns, cows, housesmoke, but no boats.
        Hillsides of apples, still, perfect.

Here my little boat takes the night Bay.
        One far neon light tosses, a city
people walk alone, its rhythmic
           landscape cut from marshes and cries.
On black water it is all mine, first
        beginnings, endings, love's beauties.
So when I move, it moves under me, and knows me.

Black Silhouettes of Shrimpers

Grand Isle, Louisiana

Along the flat sand the cupped torsos of trash fish
arch to seek the sun, but the eyes
glaze with thick gray, death's touch
already drifting these jeweled darters.

Back and forth against the horizon slow trawlers
gulp in their bags whatever rises
here with the shrimp they come for.
Boys on deck shovel the fish off

like the clothes of their fathers out of attics.
Who knows what tides beached them,
what lives were lived to arrive just here?
I walk without stepping on any

dead, though it is hard, the sun's many blazes
spattering and blinding the way ahead
where the wildness of water coils
dark in small swamps and smells fiercely of flesh.

If a cloud shadows everything for a moment, cool,
welcome, there is still no end in sight,
body after body, stench, jewels
nothing will wear, roar and fade of engines.

Two Dreams

Some dreams come true, some no.
—Robert Penn Warren

His face glides up out of woody pond water, shines
with Vermont sun, then slips under again,
the surface smoothing itself, glistening,
as he might say, like spittle, or the scar a wen

leaves, taken by the young surgeon, skin the rose
of blood doing its job. He looks not quite human,
one eye of glass, freckled like a trout, banded
by black tank suit and white swimming cap women

wore, long back, motion wandering, a moccasin's
stitching of water so murky it has no bottom.
I watch him climb out, pad up below maples
veiling October sky, until *bang*, a door slams.

A soft, distant closure like a shotgun, double,
the second concussion bouncing the first,
that one waking me so I start up. But no problem,
just hickory bent like birds in a wind-gust,

and in distance a hunter, alone, gazes up, shells
flung leaf-green in the underbrush the only sign
he's been here. I lay my head back down where
wine-red and golden leaves unfold and outline

the man-shape I'm growing into, a boy still.
There's a faint smell of wood-smoke, an edge
acidic as the cold of a cottage abandoned,
not book or plate, mouse-turd, or bone-cage

in the room I close my eyes and find. No fire,
on the hearth, certainly, all dead, so how
is it I lie dreaming that smoke, that place
that's Warren's, I'm sure, though I don't know

even his name when this happens. I'm sixteen,
hunting squirrels, napping in sunlight.
The Browning gun they gave me comes apart
when I break it to reload, shapes squeak and split

with all the noise I make. I see my weapon's
halves in my hands, peaceful, unwed, useless as
Mother and Father, and I wish I might understand
mistakes, bad decisions, what makes us so careless,

but I can't even say why my family's best vanished,
climbed down from the railroad's heaving cars
outside Pittsburgh, followed girls to the green sea,
then nights dreamed of wheels, orange vats of fire,

the way, here, I watched dark stepping toward me
out of the wood's heart where I knew someone was
already hunting ahead. I felt the cool of dirt near
stream-flow that stuttered, saw the sparrow's breast

heaving back all night poured against him, song
as futile as the gift I could not kill with.
What I could do was lie there trying to soak all in,
no moral, no lesson, just the way it happens if

you're in the middle of things, no guide, and nod off
only to wake, shotgunned, from dreams to the hiss
and glitter that shocks, and you have to think
something wanted it this way, and the hours pass

into years, years go, but you are always that same one
lying dry-mouthed, not a damn thing revealed
but the daylight, and you worry you won't find
the way to that place where the human smoke spills

upward into leaves quick as small hearts, and stars
look lethal, eyes in blackness, and wind combs
trees like a hungry Cyclops, and what if you
managed to jam together barrel and stock, plumb

some last recess of your camouflaged coat, find
a brass-banded shell like prayer answered?
From another dream, swim over, showered,
he shouts down to me to come inside, but words

scatter like living cartoons, then slip back, delicate
ghosts I hold in my hands, and my knife plows
up guts, breast, heart-stink. *Now!* he cries, but I
don't know what he wants, and if he is only shadow

in the corner of my eye, what could he say to me?
Dreams are odd, though. I feel myself sway here
and step through his calling to go back where I lived,
once, and lay in woods with a gun, waiting. How clear

his voice booms, footsteps press leaves, then night.
Whiskey in hand offered, he grins, tells me to row
across the impenetrable dark toward the sun.
His face, wrinkled and spotted with starlight, says *Now!*

for David Bottoms

LITTLE ODE TO THE WHEELCHAIR BOYS

Passing the school where midmorning sun casts crossfiring
    Spears through oak leaves, I stop my car to watch
Three boys in wheelchairs, bodies the kind we used to make
    With pipecleaners, heads bobbing as each scopes
The line they race for but cannot see. Before them the gold
    Hair of the special-ed teacher, like Psyche, swirls,
gold bangles electric, orbiting the wand of her hand. They
    Can't win, she knows, hearts badly handicapped,
Unless she gives them something like courage. Faces in shade,

They lunge when her skirt lifts, her fine legs part and flex up,
    Her young woman's breast dares them with *Go!* I
Watch how each brain pounds and is geared by desire no
    Man explains, no girl ignores. But what blood's
Heat will ask these to move a chest of drawers, while love
    Lays out a room, her gaze a mare's scent leaping
The edges of fields? What chance have these wheel-grippers
    With those who run and jump and shriek to win
Before these can find the line? Still, sucking breath, spit flying,

They hump the rutted school courts fearless as men who give
    Their one life for a cause. Fate's done something
Wrong enough to each they may fall, dumped by stone, or crack,
    And who's to blame? All day they give what they have.
Maybe it's her smell. Or the faint, last desire we put into them.
    Or the way next-hour's waddlers and water-heads
Light up for wheelies, the proud high-fives these charioteers
    Chain around this tall gold girl who always calls
The winner *Lover*, the one who'll go inside first, as a man does.

ON THE JOB

Two wives. The first unraveled, her skin dried,
an old dance dress. The second a yard mushroom
toppled and spattered by a mower. She was
coarse as the farm that sent her forth, winded,
a spore whirling until her edges caught some
thing to live by, and that was him. He, then
widowed, alone, took her to tour in the silver
Airstream so long parked under the gum tree,
wallowing one highway to another just to see
what was out there. They found out breath
wouldn't stay in her ample flesh. So then
he sank in his chair and gave God hell each
day that so little might thrive, the bad coffee
in his fist, his glare at the bright endless view
he would not walk again. Now I recall he was
like a sentry, stiff and fixed in whatever duty
there by the unrepairable RCA, its dim yellow
dial silent, and a painted deer hung above
that was too wrong for any wood men knew,
stacks of magazines she read for what Thoreau
might call the *real* information, and coupons
they put aside like signs of providence. Two
of them visible in the front window seemed
to wait upon every passing car. Then one.
He, with his pack of Camels came, smoked,
and was on the job, as he called it. Faithful.
I see today his steady watching kept a finch
repairing her nest, reminded the gumballs
the leaves needed replacements, and warned
a family of moles summer light was treacherous
if your head got up too high. No complaints,
he'd say, meaning he did as he was instructed,
the sun went up and down without a hitch.
Some days he'd take a break, a worker's right,
to counsel his visiting grandson on their past,

22

walking back the hills, sloughs, Potomac shades
of water they'd come down from Cumberland
when the Depression fell hard, nobody working,
Uncle Russ in jail, food stolen. Sickness, wars
that kept the headlights lidded, the house closed.
Someday with time, he said, he'd tell me all of it.
And I'd forget to call. I could count on him
always doing fine, feeding azaleas we'd dug in,
and boxwood I set straight beneath the mailbox
painted red, white, and blue to honor his son,
bosun on the USS Croatan framed between girls.
That's why it was so odd after rings and pick-up
names began to sing out of him. He'd shout for
someone dead, a life I never knew of, or whisper
he had to see certain ones about what was fixed,
obligations I couldn't catch, grim nuances. Then
he saw the first love reappear in her self-shaped
chair, its fringy arms not soiled like his, and if I'd
only rise, and stay with them, he'd say, time will
be summer all over again, tomatoes and onions
steeped in vinegar, and good cold chicken, too.
He made me see my own dead father coming
home from work. *Don't worry, don't worry—*
my grandfather's office, hugging me close,
already shorter by a foot than me, those words
I want to say but whose weight I can't swing
without him—like the toolbox he made full of
screwdrivers, gizmos, open-legged pliers given
to teach what a good man knows at a glance:
you can't learn how to feel, only want. All there
now lies rusted, dull, jammed-up, and silent
as the shrill and desperate plant whistle I want
to hear blowing again outside that window both
wives helped him face so long. I want to wave
where friends, beside him, came, and waited to go
on the job, and pace the walk, and take a last smoke.

RED DOG

We bought you for our son. Half-grown,
already your bag of skin sagged everywhere,
you fell to sleep like the dark in corners,
predictably where we wouldn't look under
wash piled and waiting, in closets, the moan
and wheeze of your easy breathing pointed
with pips and starts of other sounds, cries
rising, a chain of woof-woof-woofs soon to
decline like cars down the hill's far glide
of night where we said he might never go.
Of course he went, as with him went also you.

You dragged, then lost a bright steel chain: two tags
hung like my dad's world war loudly declared
"Red Dog," your name, our place, and that year's
shots, identities you'd shake off to wander
the possible world. I'd hear you, coming back,
my son still out looking, afraid you'd got
worse than traveler's bite on your mopy flanks.
His shoes puffed up dirt like spurts of time. You
mostly don't expect to find the lost—and yet,
hopeful, I'd shout, then sleep, then shout. Gone.
You'd wait. You'd creep like sun across the lawn,

then, with him, leap up everywhere, that Spring
of joy breaking roses, crushing mulched shoots
faithfully planted year after year, and roots
whose volunteers you watered dead. Soon we saw
he'd leave, you'd chase God knows what twitch
of spoor, and so we took your balls. You slowed.
Dirt-bedded, you had new smell. Bones fouled floors.
Squirrels reclaimed their nuts. The awful spew
of what spoiled in you, lying by our fire,
comes back to me as the vet says you've worn
out the heart that banged to sleep beside my son.

What does it sound like, I ask. The vet listens.
Once you climbed a six-foot fence, barking, one leap,
a storm of breath we loved. Now you only eat,
120 wheezing pounds, a processor of meat.
Like my dad, you face me, hesitate, then piss
blankets and floor. Deaf, eyes blank, the chain
slipped again, you're lost. You don't miss a boy's
games, nothing swells your interest, even the moon's
rattling tags I've hung above the waiting spades.
The vet claims it's time. We've let you go too far.
Calling at last, I say "Son. It's Red. Come home."

for Jeddie Smith

In Memory of Hollis Summers

Christmas Eve. Wild Turkey in my glass,
my country's finest drink, I sit remembering
the poet, plump, tall, bald, wisps of
smoke coiled from a cigarette holder.
I offer my poetry thesis. He laughs, says
"I'm a prissy man." He might have said
exact, or strict, as Allen Tate often did.
Later, as if bruised, he'd scowl, "Must you
say *beautiful eyes?*" And years later,
as if by accident, after my graduation,
he meets me in the hall, his hand out,
so I accept his almost-last manuscript
of poems, many speckled and moled
as his forehead, veined by hours
of burning tobacco, ash-dark as coffee,
each with scars of excisions, connections
looping word to word like metastacized
disease, but his steady strong heart
still visible, and what he wanted heard.
"Mr. Summers," I'd begin, despite quick
sputters of protest, refusing still to give
the *Hollis* he asked me many times to say
against the decades between us, being
in his view countrymen, Virginia
and Kentucky joined in that Ohio room
always bare, bright as the northern snow
we'd met in that first day. Like pioneers
with dangers in common. Now this one
came, I handed him his manuscript, not
wanting the grim words I had to give also,
circling like a scout back and forth at
the obvious, his love for her, the boys,
an old dog, a man's ways. But I knew
I'd been taught his truths, and now
fumbling to address what shadowed

what he was I made my clumsy cuts
and watched him stiffen bit by bit, who
every Christmas had a poem to send
I don't know how many students in the end.
Handwritten, the same long fingers
sharp as an aunt's needling memory as he
pointed and rasped. "Say the poem
as if it matters, David," he once groaned,
so I feel that distant hurt close in again,
being alone with those cold walls,
the chill that's in my hand as I try to find
today a heat that summered in his words,
beginning with *Hollis,* then reading from
the posthumous backward to the start
where I must shake his hand and say *Sir.*

FLOATERS

Thinking of you I happened to be staring past words into the
   screen's
blue when my left eye filled, its billowing like a glass globe
   snowball
a dead neighbor once offered me. Whiteness overwhelmed shapes,
   colors,
motions, all of it swirled, then settled, a thick curtain nothing parted.
The fear was like a stone you hear steadily against a steel blade.

Doctors dilated my eyes, they held special lenses so close I knew
what their lunch was, one said I would have laser work, and floaters.
I told him the Fall would be busy, but he pulled me to a room with
   machines.
"Now," he said. It was then I started to remember you, all I hadn't
   seen
crowding the memories of what we did and wished we had done.

The specialist made his laser surgeries three times, like flash photog-
   raphy,
sealing my sight, preparing me for "the buckle, a sort of hinge
   linking this side
with that one," he frowned, his finger vanishing from my good eye.
I saw pieces of flesh, fragments something unknown lets loose, drift
   in and clot
the way hair does in the tub's funneling gone suddenly still.
   Blindness,

Milton thought, made the mind judge, a place where angels live,
fog banks and stupors split by a radiance to show how poor is the
   little we are,
but I want, even now, your breast that dodges my reach, your soft
   arms lying
in bed fragrant as soap I keep dropping. I want to see your gold
   hairfall
that might be the sun, for all I know, that desire I once looked past.

★

Far off, everything remains what it has been, and nights when I pad
to the bathroom, the apartment window chilled, I see the city clear,
    I see
the struggle of our lives, once battered, to come up the sidewalk
    singing. Coins
rattle in pockets like the last hope men are given, but I can't see
    them, only
remember one I gave to, black but bleached by something terrible,

a Jack of Diamonds, split skull to chin, black, cream, joy shining
in Charlottesville, nineteen sixty-five when, gowned in June, I gave
    him change.
He shuffled off with years I have now, steps weightless, taking
    Jefferson's lawn
like a lion among gazelles. His eyes clouded but quickened, he
    seemed
to blink things out of the way, calling me Son, a boy who was

no more to him than gauze-wings at his ear, a word, a half
song in the street, and if I had called him Jack, or asked what
    troubled him,
or begged a blessing, would it have been wrong? An intrusion? Was
    he one who
came from the mists to say, words low in the throat, not me but this
other who comes after me will lead you? JFK's dead, Ali's down,

it's thirty years back when I see him sleeping in flowers, graduation
day, I remember I don't ask what happened, the pawnshop
    saxophone lies
half under azaleas, held to his belly, his naked ankles suppurating,
    hosting flies.
He has pulled himself out of morning sun where we march in
    ranks.
He sleeps, hat empty as blue sky on grass, but for two dimes

29

someone has offered, and someone has summoned the police, who
must have wanted him to live, for they rush to kneel against him.
Chrome revolvers, handcuffs, bullets glint at waist. How quickly they
    roll him
and noodle his arms back, then push him face-down so concrete grit
sprinkles little stars on his skin. I remember his eyes like bone plates,

as he begins to cry, muffled, then louder. One cop stuffs the horn
mouth-first in the pillow case Jack wrapped his head in, and slept
    on, only
now he sees, goes wild, pulling, hopping, afraid they'll take the horn,
    calling out
for his mother, his father, and suddenly he's dropped from the air,
    buried
in azalea's red, a weird seizure takes him, his arms fly and swat

the cap off the other cop who slips down, a boy my age, crew cut
flat, face sudden as an agate in water shining. It rises, hawks, spits.
Sun brightens a pearly essence that hangs under Jack's socket, on
    skin glowing
with sweat, dirt, the veined glob-weight starting to hunger for the
    earth.
It moves like an eye popped out, blind, obscene. Then slides off.

★

How long have I remembered, angry, doing nothing with my life,
inventing what I should do as if I had done it? Dreams wake me
sometimes trying to rip the cop's head with hands horned like that
    black angel.
I have gouged for sweetness in the bodies of lovers, broken words
as you lay, alone, waiting, and pine needles, deafening and silent,

said nothing, season after season, of what we should do. If time
enough to forget almost everything is what a man wants looking
    back,

why can't I leave him behind like the father a child says good-bye
    to, once,
the look on the face in the box fixed like a path walked at dawn?
Here, the cardinal quivers, with a new mate, delighting your cats.

It's not good, but it's not cancer, the doc says. No cause, no cure,
blind spots you'll have to try to look around. It's age, life, stress,
each man on his own, no cure, no drug. You can't blink some things
away, like insulin seizures, like thinking you're blind, like thinking
a man going blind with the sugar needs more than cops.

★

The first time I put a needle in my flesh I thought I felt mountains
shudder in Utah, I thought summer sweated high snow down for me.
I listened to jays and mockingbirds declare what was home and
    what wasn't,
swooping burghers who'd eat the other's children like Thyestes, then
    wake safe in
the air, hungry again. They made the pine branches tremble

the way Jack did gasping his breath in hard arias cops never liked.
He comes to your town, they keep him moving, but it's no good, he
squeals, a town square thickens with singing, people join in who
    can't believe
his horn music feels so good, they fill up his hat with coins. He's still
gone before the editorial's published. Or one witness writes a letter.

Have a good day, cops said. One remembers to tell the lunch crowd
the old geezer played the horn terrible, couldn't stand up, was sick,
and we both had on, Jesus, those dress uniforms, trying to be gentle,
    do right,
him screaming, too, he had to go, it's the law, business is business,
and he was sweatin' a ton, man. Anyway, life goes on, don't it?

★

The heart hopes so, for that, of all we know, we must believe if we
    are
to believe anything like the squibbed, shaded, slippery, sleights of
    hand our
God plays, with or without the explanation, for what is to become
    of us once
we know going on is only the last joke? Remembering, we see how
    to love
is the gamble of flowers, of words, of even a cop buying dinner

and Greyhound's window seat for an old flake who won't get lost.
I want you to come back, let me show you places life happens,
new azaleas blooming, cardinals taking five may strike up again,
a good Bordeaux blister with summer's heat, sliced tomatoes bleed.
We won't see thuggish dark cruising. I'll pretend to be young again.

If there's a good movie we can take it in, you'll say what happens.
Some I'll already know by measured words, the music of things.
You can read, put me to bed, if you like climb in with me. I'm hoping
I'll feel your breasts against my ribs. I'll sing for gold on your head.
I'll tell you about floaters, why I'm afraid, what I can almost see.

THE MOURNER'S LINE

1

"Have mercy!" you cry in the mourner's line,
three beauties you used to dream of show up,
same breasts, same ankles, same cheerful "Hi!"
like finches trapped in a still room, but what's
different is you: the Italian suit, the French silk tie.

That one you loved best has tall, snow-white hair.
The divorcee shyly smiles like a missed chance.
The widow is blank, serene as a hospital corridor.
They flutter and gasp and hope you will come
To the Fall's reunion dance, after so many years.
Everyone's coming, she sighs, except of course him.

2

Him is the dead, the face in the box we shuffle by.
He had muscles, was Cutest of the class, the clown
Whose quick words I remember zipped and stung me,
While these three danced in his arms one by one.
He wore them like wealth his kind never keep. Easy

As the grim one he married at last, and here she is,
Gloves clutching your forearm, same cold wet breath.
It should come to you what to say, with dreamed wit,
Of a self now an inside come out, jokeless and stiff,
His suit three sizes too big. Her dance was the twist.
Everyone's coming, she sighs, except of course him.

3

They coo what makes them throb on gold afternoons,
quick breathers, buzzing like insects, hearts you feel
must still pound as they did when sex was new.

The widow says he went fast. Don't they all, one adds.
When the line bumps us on, we hum old fears in tune.

I gaze upon a once-quick face that barked "Books suck!"
Behind class texts I hid Horace, Keats, Hardy, and Dylan.
What chance did I have to dance, kiss, take a drink
From shoes his angels swivelled in? I went on living.
As we must now, three graces and me, leaving for lunch.
Everyone's coming, I sigh, except of course him.

for J., M. J., M.

WISH FOR AN UNKNOWN DAUGHTER

This one conceived as marriage shattered,
the white leaf drifting over the spillway,
hovering over the wet depths, gone
as you, standing beneath mountain shadow,
feel a chill rise from where water was,

and, thinking now of that leaf, only itself
in a world of likenesses, its many buffets
from days, rasp of stone tongues, it sails
on slick euphoric skids of current turning
the lodged, crumpled husk it must come to.

But also sun's brightness, that otherwater
cream-flow to pools like a gift-bed waiting.
Is this too much to hope for her?—risen,
recognizable notes, Verdi or Mozart, one
door, a face, candles, life's rich spillage

swelling the hours, small creatures walking
over the water's care. You can see them
play themselves like instruments of love.
Well, wish or not, the horse in the meadow
scrubs his nose on posts where a mare passed.

A Married Woman

Sometimes in the skid of night I wake and hear
darkness like a thing alive, its cramping skin
closed on mine so I cannot move, can breathe
hardly better than stones made neon with speed
in deep space, and then I feel the faceless drift
of wind that comes from nowhere, an endless spin
locked in the heart like an unacknowledged self.
Sometimes my mouth opens as if the words will
fish what love has been out of that deeper dark,
a flow through all the layers we are, water
or blood. I think of the startled nerves I saw
crawl the face of a man leaving church, his fall,
the woman blinking at light, going down on his arm.

★

Flickering light in the sable leaves, shade so thick
it might be cupped in palms, weightless as the blurred
butterfly who links our lives without obsession,
drifting on the way eyes claim, its joy the least
lift and settle of things. Is it possession,
what things do to us?—the gray slate's lathe of flow
turning the creek at our ankles, water's slips
taken by air, birds, the nudging midges we
can't hold off, gnats naggy as desire. The wick
of memory burns me to aureoles, nipples,
skin, cream linen, your skirt hung on a dogwood,
a piece of green hitching a ride when you rose.
I told myself: keep this. Love's shade. Your tremble.

THE VILLEROY & BOCH SHOP

Look at the body, I said, nudging you, in love, childlike,
not on d'Hauteville but around the dark corner
where Villeroy & Boch shop windows run the block
in dreamy rooms of painted tile, shower stalls, baths,
fittings of silver, gold, and brass. It wasn't these I pointed at

but a man-sized roll of green blocking VB's doorspace,
a sack of what seemed laundry, or shroud, pillow-rolled,
lumped up, a thing splotched with seasons of color.
It was the Sunday we said we'd remarry. The sun,
I remember, boiled down that cobbled street like a fuse.

You remarked it must be hard living there, and meant,
I thought, dangerous where day is pack, unpack, pack
again, the Paris 10th, gypsies, Arabs, Asians, Turks, two
Americans mostly silent as faces on a Keatsian urn, but
words suddenly back like hope. *A chrysalis,* you said, then

kicked past pigeons, plotting the Metro to Diana's road.
All day, whatever museum we were in, or by the Seine
hustling under lopped-off trees, or with wind-shivered
café crème in shops where tourists unpeeled new
francs like words they'd never understand, I thought

of him: the furled ends, middle's bulge, the bumpy green
that looked as if not long before it held some limb.
What had flung it, violently, no warning, down?
It made me remember a thing I found as a child,
green as a leaf rolled in my palm, but something inside

staying perfectly still with terror. I wanted it to move.
I wanted to know what it was, and where from,
and how it got where I lived. I couldn't imagine
answers and it offered none, as I came, went, slept,
bathed, ate, grew. I thought in the end I had no choice,

I unfolded my bright blade and sawed up the center.
Would it sizzle into light and fly blinding as truth?
All I found was a huddle the size of my thumb, less,
a juiceless, gauzy creeper, stiff twig, an eye blank
enough you could stare forever and not see a thing.

In school they told me what it was and what made it
crawl to lay in that place, like love's will to keep going.
It was a tangle of selves it couldn't escape, a battle
that used up all the wiggle there was. It's just death,
no reason, they said, no knife words could name did it.

At Villeroy and Boch, you teased: Was it bad and ugly?
You were in a loving mood. Unravel this self, you said,
show me the past that breathes. We'll see Diana later.
But I was pushing you hard toward the Metro, not
wanting to say what this man meant, wanting to go

where life flashed with glamour's old secrets, the Latin
Quarter and Moulin Rouge. I wanted to believe the love
that once lifted winged creatures over roofs and roads
could keep alive Winter's man, one kept so perfectly
still by toilets, bowls, and glass breasts at Villeroy & Boch.

                                        for Dee

PLANTING

Valentine's Day, 1999

This time last year green-smocked workers swept
the Tuilleries path smooth as carpet readied for love's
invading guests, and we passed, hand in hand, by trees
pruned slim as Pigalle's nude dancers, few birds but you
singing as day woke in that gray. Dogs walked women
in Seine shadows hunched under Winter's grip,
but shop fronts wore buckets full of brilliant blossoms
as if some war went on I hadn't seen. You wanted

to walk, fetched by a dream that color gave, and made
me rise where pigeons crowded a saint's arms, our steps
climbed Sacré Coeur's hill, Montmartre's mazy alleys
wound us, left us to pant at inward, enticing doors
latched hard by the cold we tramped as if we'd been
Roman poets, or Irish lovers, exiled, clenched on a hill's
cobbly flank, huddled from all the ice, wind, words
that locked us in rooms we fled, and forgot. Today

our thirty-third Spring reminds me how Paris sun
sent windows snicking up, and drew forth the moans
of door-darks, and song. Then green flecked all over,
finches in clearest blue the eye knows swooped close.
At Joyce's Tavern and La Lapin Agile good, cold beer,
soft dusks; we picked a budding vine along the hill's
wrong side, to grow we said when we were home,
a savory flag of what would not give up on us. Easter

came, went, hot days, streets gagged by tourists, home
words our own, surly in that sweet light grown longer.
They spoke to us as memory does, so loud we fled.
Now winter's night fades; birds peck seed we drop.
You paint another room Monet's yellow, I push
a shovel in and out, the sound just Paris breathing
hard, or maybe hearts amplified where people walk
recalling luck and love until it's time to plant and bloom.

39

NEW ORLEANS ENGAGEMENT

First shivers of palm fronds lift over the French Quarter.
Hurricane's coming through courtyards, alleys,
beating the pompon clusters of oak leaves to convulse
then wheeze and catch a breath. Pieces of grit,
green, gold, swirl up at the eye, sparkly as Mardi Gras
gifts flung against doors, and now clouds
blackpile and whisk by, as if all's changed, the world's
putting on the blue of evening, a sickly green
wads the laketop, and the sky's got yellow veins. Here's
enough to make you see what fear is, all you
can do about it, too, so I swing with a grip on a tumbler
of Jameson, sweeping my watch where
a fence-top swears beauty won't last, flowers fly apart.
I'd like to have eyes that don't miss a thing
but I'll settle for bigger shapes, the feeling a storm brings
as it gains weight, like love, shoving, thrashing
Ponchartrain's placid waters to froth and lap, neither salt
nor whatever's not. This marsh stays dangerous.
As any big breather knows, life's a shallow
bowl, so I want to know what's what, get my boat
where my fingers don't have to dig in deep wood. You can
see what people's faces look like once the spray
spreads its egg-white all over, you can say what warmish
sluices sag in their underwear. The days I love
break and bring me to see you cooking red beans, rice,
maybe cornbread, too, hair all wispy, sound
of wind and things falling what I hear, so I make my song.
I catch you coming, barefooted, to the door,
worry's music faint, in the skin of your dress, and I think
how those in the boats are thinking this is the last
of everything, last trip away from the house, last redfish,
last memory of good luck, last chance to say
Please, God, I love her or that *Please* that doesn't know
the end of its thought. Like me, when I see
you pouring the Bordeaux, who called and asked me to come

home for the storm that wants us to eat alone,
or not at all, and is shaking the trees like a voodoo spirit
saying not here, not now, maybe not tomorrow.

No Stars on the Water

Our daughter's dog leaps and spins in the surf
of water where our ordinary yard used to be
just hours ago, before rain like time pushed in
with first sizzle of mist, then wind's uncertain
gasps, a big boomer breaking it open like a kiss
unexpected, so the puppy's part is nerve-struck

joy, romping, splashing, the bad noise still far off
we know, now, will come. A torrent silvers down,
boils over the roof, swizzles through fisted leaves,
a mud-dappled amniosis spreading out of darkness
suddenly swollen, lightning like a flashed secret,
and the wiggly panic like the knife a child waves

in the school play where parents cheer and weep.
We wanted that kind of pride, a small body's
happy pouring forward, breath's yearning to take
each next step, however deep or gleam-blinded.
Nothing tests love like fear and joy. I hear you
tuck in a child upstairs, as she hears the rain

softened by walls. Her face will lift, look confused
with each near noise, then settle, comforted by
what hangs close, and known. Here, I shudder
with the sky's cutoff, last blips plunking a cold
skiddy surface so unnatural I feel sliced inside
when your gaze lowers and your voice goes

spattering against my fingers like ache's shredding
that couldn't be held back any longer. The dog
comes unremembered, shakes, a spray like words
chilling, all that has been flung out now, weight
enough we turn from it, like someone's crying
last wish I'd shut the door on the night, as I did.

From *Fate's Kite* (1996)

ARISING

Did he peek like a child where nippled sunlight poured,
did he call from cradling dark a woman to come,
did he brush off gravel, aware of himself,
did he sing in his skull despair as men now do,
did he first unfill what swelled his lower parts,
did he hear that water blooming like her breath,
did he know which way up held his face, his feet,
did he fit his palms where the rock must answer,
did he fight the poison of desire's first bite,
did he smell what the rock held out as well as in,
did he consider rituals, duties, days ahead,
did he say to them your best clothes are useless,
did he tell the first face I have missed you most?

FIDDLERS

Black mudbank pushes them out like hotel fire.
Some at water's edge seem to wait for transport.
Others sweat, pale, scattered on the shining beach.
All keep closed the mighty arms of God's damage,
waving at shadows and movements made by the sun.
Desire, the dragging arm, sifts, picks, tastes, untastes
endlessly the civic occasions the tide brings in.
Surely floods, cold fronts, embolisms of dreams
drive them in where the earth's brain hums. They
clasp, breed. They glare upward in rooms where the moon
slips its question. Daylong they spout, fume, command.
Biblical as kinsmen with a son they must kill.
Nouns, verbs couple like years. Water comes, listens.

OLD COUNTRY

Why had nobody told me they'd be the words
I'd worked with since birth, and the mouth's makings
showed that flash of good teeth, that bloody tongue
all we could claim? Women so fair and upright
we made them angels in stories of killings
nobody could do as well as we had. The beards
our fathers wore surfaced among these and stunned
with thickness and length. Like crabs in the pot,
layered, making salute to death, they bubbled
and clacked and clung hard to each other's darkness.
I felt at home under the tall clock's rumble.
You had to look close to see how this business
meant to explode each sweet face and changeless heart.

WRECK IN THE WOODS

Under that embrace of wild saplings held fast,
surrounded by troops of white mushrooms, by wrens
visiting like news-burdened ministers known
only to some dim life inside, this Model
A Ford like my grandfather's entered the earth.
What were fenders, hood, doors, no one washed, polished,
grazed with a tip of finger, or boyhood dream.
I stood where silky blue above went wind-rent,
pines, oaks, dogwood ticking, pushing as if grief
called families to see what none understood. What
plot of words, what heart-shudder of men, women
here ended so hard the green world must hide it?
Headlights, large, round. Two pieces of shattered glass.

A Lay of Spring

My father must have been cold in his casket,
ice shocking the Bermuda lawns, roads, tulips
just trying to get born. I wanted him alive.
I dreamed, I yelled. I was sorry, seventeen,
not yet a man, brooding believers, a nonsmoker.
He left quick as his sizzled Pall Malls, wordless.
I kneeled with the heavy Baptists who prayed hard.
Then quiet, tulips came red, yellow, boozy sun
welding my eyes. The time I passed out was May.
This is my song. He's gone. I begged let me be
touched, for tomorrow I'll only grow older.
Alice fed me mountain oysters. Summer started.
Buds dropped. Alice swelled. Preaching? Poetry? You lose.

Blowfish and Mudtoad

Held the wrong way either will take the finger
that clamps the casual pen, changing your words,
its rows of teeth like a serrated bread knife.
Moss-covered as bottom rock, wearing the brown
scum of salt water settlers, current-fluttered
flags of weed, eyes like glass pitted by age,
each reads steadily the downdrifted offerings
its tongue ticks for: crawlers, wings, limbs, all
the great current gathers to sweep away at last.
Our line sinkered into that steep wants a sleek
one to claim us—big Blue, Striper, Thor-like Drum.
Not these nibbling small-town preachers, Mudtoad's
black ambush, or Blowfish, resurrection and rage.

THE GODS IN MY BELLY

Some nights the katydids cease, holding their breath,
waiting, and razzing racket of August heat
sinks down, filling me like insucked air when love
lifts your face suddenly before mine. It gives
that shudder along the spine, the knife-through-meat
feeling you have when the doctor brings his touch.
Under long-armed black oaks and the pine's limp brush,
green lizards blow out pink macho throats, then wait.
Far off, blanched, glistening in this same moonlight,
swells slapping where the ocean seethes in distress,
something flays with long teeth a bloody other,
the small gust of lung's last comes, a heart flutters.
Stillness and fear walk inside me, night listening.

THE LOUISIANA SEA OF FAITH

This land lies low toward the Gulf, a ridge
halved by the Mississippi, abandoned
where great sturgeon, shark, turtles loomed,
our daily rising mist the last letting go,
breath's rot fertile enough to root the lush
cycling of the short-lived and the hopeless.
Twice annually our people cry out and binge
for lives drained in the torque of a death
that clings like sodden summer shirts: Mardi Gras,
Christmas balance priests and bare-breasted women.
The winter sun yanks orchids from the darkness.
Men drift past the levee like beer cans, our mothers,
our daughters rasp "Throw me something, Mister."

ELEGY FOR MY FRIEND'S SUIT

He saved all year for the gray suit, Brooks Brothers,
because he wanted the best, but left unworn
what the plastic shroud held. All night I watched, drank,
who outlived him by years. Tempted, I armed it.
Two blocks away surf rolled; sky and ocean kissed.
Waiting to be him, not yet poet of joy and time
I danced in surf, a 42-regular.
I stunk up dawn, puddled floors, left heaped seaweed.
His dead face still laughs when I ooze from that sun,
that squint he had from birth a friend's blink at truth.
His eyes went kingly. Women squirmed to touch him.
That kiss of death on his arm sighed "what a prick."
"But well-suited for dancing," he said, "though less than we."

NINE BALL

My anger's long for the room of broken chairs in rows,
spittoons with death's brown beauty breeding its glue
atop the stairs that clattered and turned you in
where they waited, shot, glared, and hooted, the goons
who knew more ways to make you "Rack and Pay" than
Pilate's birds in dusk's dark trees. I took my cue
hour by hour, learning what deceit is, the tuck, throw,
and cushion lean you'd need if they missed the break.
Nearsighted, I kept losing the paths they'd spin.
Then the shooters faded to just faces along the walls,
only tales in pieces, whispers. Then I bent alone.
They took all I had with a greased game of nine ball.
Come tomorrow, they said. I meant to. I still mean to.

ALMOST AT SEA

Morning light pours through our rented, busted slats,
thick enough we float on it, a baby oil
whose sweet smell is yesterday's Fritos and Coke.
It makes you sweat along the brow to wake here,
the air like a boat's bow upside down in May.
And yet faint like those fingers on your hips,
desire's nibbling, that old friend, begins again.
Can you feel bobbing out-tides bump, crazy shrieks
from bombing birds that can't outfly their small lives?
I want to lie long where your legs drift apart,
listen to the freight's far coming rumble,
feel the sun's buoyant resurrection slip
beneath us, lift us, and kiss the good years back.

MAKING A STATEMENT

Thousands, lately, have asked me about my hair.
Why is it so long? Why haven't you cut it?
I think about Samson, of course, and his woe.
His hair like thickets where I was born, swamps,
tall grasses bending with red-winged blackbirds
like a woman's nipples in the quick sun-gold.
I could tell about Samson, about the girl,
but I say my head is cold. I need cover.
Playing tennis with a leggy blonde I love,
I admit I can't do anything with it, my youth.
She rolls her eyes into a smashing serve.
"You old guys," she teases with her hot drop-shot.
Back and forth all day, yellow balls, long gray hair.

Boys in the Square at Bologna

Across the courtyard of gold fountains at dusk
they strut, water lifting like smoke from penises
of stone. The dark earth cools as each one
preens in the square's mouth, indolents, masks,
beringed fingers, pigeons cooing for secrets
of the centuries oozed like spilled milk.
When our girls come on silky heel clicks, three
whistle up the air's exotic cries. They bob
like fish white for the moon, and leap. Some disrobe,
chests pale as panties, big neckchains, amulets
dancing, Marlboros, scooters' razz. The loudest
spout louder what fucking they will do tonight,
their hands miming the untouched and ripe.

Lunch

Hours of tapping keys and staring, sullen clouds
the morning's mood all scud and bump, hold
and go, images of what's unknown, yet wanted,
dissolving so the sun appears, the gloom yields.
The shade is cold but the courtyard's filled
with flume of light, the soul's warm surround
I bring my lunch to: Vienna bread homemade,
local cheese, its wedged hunks like marigolds
yellow and sharp, bologna's muscle added,
and mustard to make the eyes weep, and beer,
beaded Dutch, a fistful of chips, an orange
deftly sliced so, unbruised, inner light's let out.
Crows struggle with their rhymes. I eat, all ears.

FANTASTIC PELICANS ARRIVE

Gray wind across the lake's back comes raking,
tiny sails of white foam, crest after crest,
sun beating like neon against cold's waves,
solitary loon floating in the cove. Today
the good bankers, egrets and angular herons,
keep hours elsewhere, sure of trouble's weather.
Yet clumped in a wide white pod that bobbles,
cell by cell swirls, spooks out, then returns, some blind
trajectory coiling back like bad blues: pelicans
overnight blown in, desire's floaters, fat boys
seining the shallows for something still hidden.
We runners stop, whisper. They honk in joy,
sleek hens and gullet-swollen middle-aged monks.

AUDUBON AND CHA CHA

Bent, opened, on my back for the new hygienist,
watching Audubon's brown pelican, its gaze
startled as if she's recognized me, I see
she looks vengeful, obsessed, beak stuffed. "I'm Cha Cha"
say plump hands in my mouth quick to muscle down
where the days have weakened my stiffest root.
She probes and pricks. The wall clock ticks. Her blade scrapes.
Half-moon earrings chime against my cheek.
"So how's this feel?" Gagged, I watch, grunt, and nod OK.
Death hides from bird eyeballs, and mine, day bright as a tooth.
I feel her moves as machines keep the room cool.
I taste my blood. Her breasts bell like lilies.
Praise Audubon. Praise pain. Praise Cha Cha today.

NATURE MOMENT

Dusk, when he jogs, he asks himself, Is this it?
Lake flat as rolled sheet steel, God's orange and purple
sky like a Cadillac never garaged, ruining
fumes still hung while the music maker rolls on.
Fish boil up. The paper says they're distorted,
too many fins, too few. He thinks Evolution?
Macadam hurts his feet, but doc warns the heart
needs rotation like his tires. That smashed turtle
he asked his mom, years back, how to fix—what made bleeding?
She returns, then, like light in ligustrum's thick scent.
What was her smell? Kids rocket past, pealing laughs,
jittery last-minute finch calls from hairy darks.
Why make this turn? He knows bush, house, but no reason.

ANOTHER NATURE MOMENT

My Deep South, still famous for heat, lassitude,
hospitality, and mannerly ways of
keeping its big gut-wrench with the past hidden,
unless you can read, or fail to notice trash
gets swept away one side of town, yet adorns
the other: we're paralyzed. An invasion
of Yankee air TV claims has cracked our borders
spills its tingling brittle little mirrors all
over magnolia, azalea, marigold,
banana palm, hibiscus, and clinging rose.
Our ladies step out, damage assessors, down flagstone,
and lift shards of ice from dirt they treat like kin
and toss aside that dark face, and smile like the sun.

DAILY MESSENGER

After tennis with Big Deal, the visiting poet,
sets halved, my slicing shots quick as couplets,
and greasy burgers with beer, for which he treats,
clouds shrink, gray scuds off like ship silhouettes
vacuuming all griefs; buttery sun oozes out.
I drop off thirteen shirts, no starch please,
then find a man by the car, voice a low pout.
"Man," he says, "I got no cash. I got needs."
His shirt is Polo, the little horse on left
tit a giveaway, his shoes pricey Nikes.
Suddenly I see my shirts hung, darkly wet,
as if I've died on the court, he's come for me.
He's black, in whites perfect for the tournament.

WRECKAGE AT LAKE PONTCHARTRAIN

Baton Rouge to New Orleans, hauling Route 10,
workweek done, flying home with old tunes booming,
road jolts, shaken by the bodies revealed,
I come into the room of a long wood quiet
as parlors. Wisps of moss like an elder's beard.
I fly by two frightened grandmothers glancing
from a Chrysler. Miles on I'm shamed by the glare
of their pouchy lipsticked fear, a melted look
I see at malls. Whose is the law of the eyes?
I turn loud Chuck Berry's "Go Johnny Go," pop
my beer, grin, alive. Then I slow down to watch
the ageless, dead lake, a carpet stinky, black,
giving under cranes who step ashore alone.

Water Pitcher

Racks of green, long spout, rubbery plastic, the kind
stacked in tall edgy ranks in the Garden place
back at Kmart, set up for use, for Spring's birth.
They seem to say things need digging, get out pal.
They make you wonder what hand's been planning things.
Today my wife's placed hers to catch some rain,
but skies seem endless as the future of grass
that climbs on its own. Who says flowers need us?
It sits where the gutter's busted. Will rain spill,
tapped to deeps she knows, better water that sprays
at her hand like love poured on what needs it most?
That I understand, my drinking in her years.
But what moon-surfing force holds the sun? What mind?

Palm Trees at 1430 Knollwood Drive

Yul Brynner might make an entrance under them, brass
breastplate flashing, that famous skull nicely soft
where fronds wash the humid air for hard-eyed folk.
They're regal as deacons on the Baptist steps of
resurrection day with the light pink, unwicked
for once, the other trees in greenest essence
as befits a chorus, a cardinal's flame trumpet
surging precisely in domestic suites of notes.
For years I've moaned I can't write God's poems
but now I see the sentry palms laugh like men,
and each rattles a single fist of annual fruit,
small and dark gold, an emblem hissing Praise me!
In brief bursts everything does, this Easter Sunday.

ONE HUNDRED TWENTY-NINE DOLLARS

The law says you can dig the hole or buy it.
July, heat same as Louisiana's usual barbecue,
I take the axe to chop my boxer deeply in
and whack and whack and whack three clay inches,
an hour's sod, task for eight hours I calculate,
wheezing, sweating like an emphysemac. Crowns
of dust rise on weed-leaves, a golden nimbus
I must be smoking as I hack, chip, and gouge
what God's word says we'll all end up in.
The bloated body, wrapped in his old rug, waits
awake, it seems, when I stop, black eyes watching.
The vet's hole costs $1 per pound, so I pay.
Fouled, barked over, the room of the world stinks.

IRISH WHISKEY IN THE BACKYARD

Two dwarf oranges, one tangerine, one grapefruit,
rescued from Kmart's clearance sale, leafless souls,
luminous with Louisiana sun, volts
near liquid, rare buds of white like a woman's part,
the soft oily leaves it takes a long time to
open to peak conception, which is work, fate,
or luck good as orphans get. December's blush
here might be Christ's happy gaze spilled, not salt
lapping every road up north, not cold house-ache,
not winter's bloodless shuffle past dark and light,
faces like roadside toads, flashbulbed and stunned.
But who knows what happiness is? I drink and stroll
and night comes cool as years in our green suburb's clamped vaults.

THE PENUMBRAL LEGACY OF HUEY P. LONG

There's an election here every week. Life's costly.
The boys stand for judge, commissioner, or school board.
We give them sweet syllabic schoolyard filth to hurl
if the fools are brave enough to walk our streets.
Years back we tossed rocks. Now it's automatics.
We're beswirled by Nike Airs, Polo running suits;
we' got chains, stocks; we could easily be kings.
We're impressed by all the world can give, kicked back,
fresh girls daily, unburdened by work that stinks.
We've voted ourselves big dicks, fast cars, no dying.
We've dropped your blossom-buried back fence like pants.
We've thrown your people out. We'll tax your sins, we'll sue.
We've got the votes to change things the southern way.

QUAIL

Recalling old hunts, we rake ourselves with hooks
of briars along the bottom where a dog's stiff.
Field seeds fleck our cracking lips like blood, mouths
moving every step, taking sky, limbs, and weir
birds break from all at once. One won't come out.
It stamps and clucks and waits in death's little room.
"Bit by bit the world fans away . . . ," I hear your poem.
But what part's ours? I'm hefting my grandfather's gun
first time in my mind. It slams me back, like age.
Now stinkbird flutter. Tired, we chat and walk, pained
we've only knocked from air words. All flies faster.
Gloom makes us kick dark-gathered bush, then harder.
To hold our dogs, we coo and chime "Whoa, dead here."

for Charles Wright

STALLED ON THE EBB TIDE

Out against the darkness, against absence, strokes
glowing in what is not light, exactly, plank by plank
we push ahead into freshets and shudders
of water, black time glinting. The boat rocks
but holds, for now, what we put into it,
flesh, blood, the smell of sex. How did we become
what water wanted more than earth? We are dregs
of things, last flickers bobbing, out of the fire
of the sun floating the good days, unclaimed,
as pure as seaweed. If we cry to the stars,
thrown free of waves, what hope thin as finned crusts,
belly up, ichthyic, can beach us in night's small skiff?
Piece and piece and piece going by. Moonstuffs.

CANARY WEATHER IN VIRGINIA

It comes in sharp, salt smell above James River's foam.
It clatters past azalea, willow, the exhumed sway
Of laurel, camellia's pink-smoked buds dawning open,
Oiling a woman's hands to spill moonlight in woe's rooms.
It flings unseen to anywhere he lives bands of wind
Unfolding so many gold birds dawn sings with god-breath.
Yellow-red streaks pass like her hair over his pillow.
What mission has it in droughty fields, uncoiling faith
That remembers to bring also cardinals, owls, gulls?
Swamp-sheen, a dew-gilt mast, mullet's leap, cold horse-eye
Lift, hold him up, though he stiffens, alone in his yard.
When tides wash distance in, he floats, fate's kite, back
To silhouettes of pine, boats, that whirling yellow bird.

A Gift for Seamus

What could I give you back but slate-toppling waves
white-cropped now like you, wearing in and onward,
steady as the manhood of the heart? Friend, slaked
by dippers of words you've drawn for thirty years, I
find myself yet pulled by aching thirst for bursts
against the sunlit shore, that deeper black cold
welling up from somewhere bottomless like hurts
we've hidden under memory. You've the great feel
of things, broken faces, glint of what's best said by
gull-swoop, glance, the look down in that's a cry
unmade but by the delicate tongue of the gifted.
In me the chapped, sloshed underpool holds the sway
your singing makes, my gift to listen and to nod.

Descending

Remember that tin-foil day at the beach descending
on water the color of slate, the man descending,
just a bald head like an emptied melon descending
God knows where, same day a shy girl-child descending
with doll and bike to darkness where, descending
the hill with dumptruck vizor down, sun descending,
a father squints just once and the years descending
ever now spin him like a pump's flush-pipe descending
to pure waters he can never reach and, descending,
what of wings flamed gold, dusk's holy glow descending,
heron, tattered, wearied, news-heavy head descending,
that's left by hunters to float all night, descending
as they do into sleep, the earth clean, just descending?
Where, and with whom, are those we've seen descending?

From *Cuba Night* (1990)

Writing Spider

A path coils like the aphid's gouging the rose,
a dark line lingering by the finger beans.

No one sees me outrun the whiskered corn
or spill myself on the grass
or fall amazed under her silken staring.

Electric against the black law of the trees,
huge yellow zigzags around her
like lightning. A mystery, I think.

There's not yet the evidence we expect, swaddled
stingers, fuzzy cocoons well prepared—
but for whom? The web glistens.

I see the trunks leaning in, as if she draws them
with her tiptoeing strength. I rise,

pulling myself from under her without touching
or being touched, clothes a little clammy.
How old am I when I lift the stick,

prod this and that corner of her concentration?
It requires her to type back and forth
her swaying, signing possession.

I get very close and I do not believe
she has come to this revelation for me.
Or that she can jump

from time to time.

CRAB HOUSE

Noon at the swamp's heart, the stink
falling from the smokestacks
cloaking the slender reeds that do not move.

Workboat's kapucka-kapucka pushes
the dark wave in over the mud,
then pulls it back so the skulls shine.

A gull settles onto a distant swell,
picks at white feathers like a German maid
in a sun-dappled bed. The sound of many legs

scraping against metal, the sound of water
boiling is in this air. I listen
as the swamp grinds its teeth, feeds, begins to reek.

2000

It's always been nineteen something for me.
Nineteen for my father all his life,
nineteen for my grandmother who went,
nineteen for my sister who wanders,
nineteen for my grandfathers who won't make it,
nineteen for my wife who will, our children,
and, for all I know, yours, and theirs.
Nineteen is a lot of sad, dirty numbers
and something that reports to none of us.

What good are words in the face of numbers?
They keep the shadow under a boat rotting
where I crawled as a child, they hide
the pitted spoon of dreams, they deliver
wind in tunes over the reed-heads of home.
They turn my father's face to a thin plank
where I cross the creek over fallen stars.
They are the zeroes of sorrow something says.

I want to pick up my ears like a tired dog
when the whistling comes over the fences.
I want to lie down and dream of God counting
my sins until in anger he sounds sexual
as a Peterbilt diesel in a fishing scow.
I want to watch the words: nineteen something.
They'll loop out of sight like a slow worm
and I won't even try to read the slime,
the dirt, or the revolutions of the moon.

TREADING CLAMS AT EGG ISLAND

Among us the fathers labored like seals
and we would come behind them, crotch-
deep, tiptoeing the motherly waters,
each naked foot kicked out where sand
humped, darkness hiding its treasures,

then body's tumble and thrust to make
the fetal coil, to begin a weightless
grope downward through broken swells
of milky bottom. Opening the eyes,
we'd see weed-hair, polyps, big legs

before the salt's burning poured through
nerves and brain-stem. We'd convulse
head first from a shimmering cleft,
new muscles threshed by sun, matted
with the dead cells of old bar spawn.

Afternoons, floating with baskets, we
were catchers of the living and the dead
alike, oblivious, churning forward as
the tide washed us to a smell of dirt,
our lank place they called an island.

We learned to breathe hard and steady
as we opened them, knife-bulling,
the dangerous shove that risks slips
to the bone, praising the smaller,
least salty cherrystones not long

fallen from current's spurt and swell.
Walking over our people's garbage,
we'd gather to boast, to lie into fires
hidden by the cradles of sawgrass.
Houselights winked where water ended.

Fingering each mysterious seam, ridges
readable as a family line, grown
sleek, we were the muscles we loved.
Whatever we opened told us of more
out in the black water, so we plunged

to find the firm, sweet, angelic flesh,
scaring ourselves with the moon-steam
of our diving. Then, calling to stars,
the brothers of creation who made us,
singing aloud for the life we lifted up,

the salted, pink-lipped, slimed pumpers,
we grew sea-clotted, our stenchy skins
scaled and shining, and passed nightyards
with old boats lying moon-weighted, open
as if they were dreams unfinished. There, we

stood like our fathers. Our baskets down,
we'd fight some, shout the dead awake.
We would wait. Already there'd be women
afoot in the levels of darkness, stirred
to venerate what we caught, what they caught.

PILLAGE

The sun has done eternal damage, pine warped
to the white, arthritic shins of men. Here
they shouldered hung come-alongs and galled
harnesses, they led out the heavy striders
of meadows and later stood counting the green
strings of hunger as they passed the tall door.
Here are roofholders they raised, gray beams
axed from an infinite country's brood, and ribs,
struts, planks, overlapped, darkened by time.
Against the back wall startled wings beat,
noting our presence, stirring the rich silts
of the world that lives here now, the silence
unmocked by our loud crying out. In a frieze
of webs a shadow moves and we feel ourselves
placed in shafts of light, trespassers driven
from desire to fear in this abandoned barn.
Why are we here? we ask aloud, as if the dead
wood knows, unimpeachable as nests of swallows.
But even Prince Albert stays speechless, canned
at dirt-shrouded windows we can't budge. What
do we want badly enough to risk this stealing
under the cathedral roof? Something black seems
alert above as we back toward the August light
and pass beyond the scaled foundation stones
handlaid like a language we once understood.
Once out we are chilled in the sun, the smell
of ourselves oddly imprecise yet powerful
as a memory of passion when we stand alone
remembering how we crept in, how we burst out,
our hands filled with cowbells, straps, tools,
relics for mantels in our bright, modern houses.
Agreeing to return some Sunday, already we
make up tales to explain why we never go back.

WELDERS

Behind us, at the window, my grandmother
stood with death's fat melting her down.
Today all I have of her is the stone
grave, the ground we loved for pines
swaying through hammered Sunday sermons.

Here the booming day-long traffic darts
like just-dead souls embarking, spits
of light from windshields burning away
the last green where she was put in.
That summer they meant to teach me desire

would lead to lingering pain, blindness,
the cost of making things go together.
I stood near grandfather's dark place,
full size in fig's shadow of green,
still as an acolyte, his pricking stream

of light motes turning the world in my head
molten as July's flare. "You look aside,
you'll see. . . ." But I disobeyed and stared.
Black-cowled he hunched, became a monster,
a gargoyle scowling, a bent breath-sizzler

whose hands cradled swamp-fog and fire.
Was this the chest I had slept on
to hear the histories of our names?
A nerve in my brain turned phosphor
until I went faint among the needles.

What was he making? Rabbit-trap, the last
beauty-catcher for her? The bright gutter
she watched, the spurt and lick of life
blistering those who gaze into black
distances—that's all we keep. In a heap

somewhere whatever it was still moulders,
not the astonishing moment of a maker's
clang and bang of vision. Nothing.
Then the hand touching. How much?
I imagine the faces who look at it,

blank, as if all is only to be embedded
in silence, ignorance, season's passage.
As if knuckles of steel did not speak.
Days then her hands cooled my forehead.
Light sizzled and we went on, making.

LAKE DRUMMOND DREAM

For we are not pans and barrows . . .
—Ralph Waldo Emerson

Reading Emerson. Cottonmouths are moving mildly
in swamp midden, the whip
of nerve-spurred flesh
going down, glints

incidental in the rolling fume of darkness
where the moon fingers like thought
and eases around the rib cage
of beauty. To find life

in the eye's cleavage: a spread spiraling water
gone still, sudden. Puddle in backyard,
the standing scum. Depth unexpected
in all things, the striking

quickness of the afternoon overhead, remembered,
and not to be able to confess the name,
the nature of what marries all.
Then, the self sitting

stiller than the sparrowhawk inside his glance,
already owning, without awareness,
small wings. Dreaming of home,
the lake, spine-sliders,

not expecting to touch, across the library desk,
a woman's hand, finding it dry, cool,
eyes shocked open, all
the darkness around

uncurled from deep texts of matter. Know it comes,
hear, touch time's announcement. Plant

the feet on the floor's waterskin.
Try to know the unavoidable

thing, meeting its depth.

On Looking into Neruda's *Memoirs*

At the end of Elliewood Avenue one black night
the police came whirling batons
to crack heads and leave
the students in the seeping flush
of camellias that Spring.

A woman found me and into the riot we went, me
tugged by the ghost-tendril of her arm,
bolting by the tidy lawns until down
we lay at the serpentine wall,
panting, in new music

beating from an open window—"The Famous Flames"
maybe, but she was cool, wordless, alert
as a dove to the night noise.

She uncradled her hungers in the dark, then rose
lank as the poet Gabriela Mistral,
whom Neruda saw in his youth.
He called her gray stick,
as if she were the heron
owning the world with icy steps.

Why has she waited to enter this poem, a small
scald at my brain's back?
Whatever she put in my hand
was grim and hard in the heaving.
Go on, show them, she said, *give them a taste.*

She hovered on the corner, a tall shadow.
When they came to beat me she stepped away
through helmeted heads, a saint
with an eye of disdain
for all my earnest words.

It doesn't matter, the dutiful life, the poems.
A man will complain for his first loves,
brick smell, lost village, sexual
odor of swamps, the scarf
of a nightwalker, a single camellia.

Mistral, who worshipped the long-stick God
of the Crusaders, kneeled in the huts
where Neruda grew. He saw her
once, enough,
a stick making poems.

Bitch, you almost hear him hiss,
pressing her hard in the story of his life.

CAMELLIAS

Something with claws, with trap-spring teeth
honed, shining where leaves peel
back from midnight's folds,
is intent and desperate beyond
the imagination where I look,
howled awake: a few
luscious petals suddenly are shaken,
so I think guilt always
keeps just behind the heart.
In beauty something is jerking a small other
apart, breaking the slight bones,
the cross-stitched sinews,
its tongue drawn like a shaving knife, abandoned
where it hunches. Nothing answers
either, only the silence hiding
the scream that came,
pitiful as the nightmare in the ear
of the lover. It is
no decent hour but I ease from my bed's cool,
step down the blind corridor
with my nakedness swaying, then
paw for the switch. Harms I might do rise
like a fester of wings when I throw
the light of revelation over our backyards,
into bedrooms. What makes me
heave it as indifferently as a hunting sun?
Instantly something clenches
the earth, digs in, doesn't
bolt, lifts itself to see, mouth partly open,
the tiny tongue in throat-black,
and throat as well, disguised but pink
as the unfolded, dewy crenelation
of camellias uncountably opening
themselves in seasons

pure as Florida. It is all framed
by the flawless black meat and fur coiled
upon itself like night–after–night.

CUBA NIGHT

The small of the back has its answers
for all our wrong turns, even the slightest,
those aches there's no name for, or source,
and the mole in the mirror, a black moon
of sudden importance, can turn your hours
into love's rapt attention. As you shave
an innocent glance into the yard pulls
your lips mulishly—is anything there
more than a choice, a will to live? When

the fly on its back, feet up in dead air
between the storm-doubled panes, stiffens
it seems a reminder redolent of a word
you can't speak, like history, but feel
as once you felt the shuffle and slap
of your father's feet on heartwood floors.
He would be bathed then, as you are now,
unshirted, coffee starting, his lathered
clownish cheeks white, the dawn oozing red.

Quizzical, you hear the razor pull closer,
strokes deliberate, hard, almost independent.
Is it death? Only a café memory, you two
standing outside, soft night, a radio,
Kennedy declaring over the dirt his one
line only a war could cross. Your mother
wasn't yet meat that a drunk's Ford would
leave in a frogspawn ditch. Then your father
stopped to visit, shy, held your teenage hand,

while along the block many leaned, listening.
Dusk steadily bled all the light from each
face, a voice—maybe Bob Dylan's—said this
is history, and you said what? Same word
when your wife cried I can't stand any more,

whose crying had started under your yes, yes.
You can't smell her stale sheets and no
memory's kiss mushrooms. No late show's
rerun of Bikini atoll keeps flaring at you.

What then? Only azaleas beginning to explode
that must have been planted in that year,
the smudged hand now earth's, with questions
he couldn't answer. His eyes brimmed wetly.
Nobody you know's been to Cuba or cries out
what history means. There's blood on your lip.
The mole has grown. You're starting over,
remembering the floor that seemed to shake
with their love, then your body slipping free,
her nakedness, soap-white. Then the shaving.

A PINTO MARE

Mud packing her gullet the robin pecks
at winter-withered grass, black eye
cocked, serene as a man I saw bent
at a radar screen's blipless blue. His
lips spread on a mouthful of pizza
as the end of the world settles, a joke
I took home when my duty was done. Now

just beyond my window the thunder booms
Spring at this scruffy, fearless bird.
There's no worm and no nest in sight—
what makes her keep on, rain misting
through trees slick as missiles? She
rips, skips, tears hunks of the earth,
a nerve dutifully alert to what day is.

Years ago, just married, I walked with
sun napalming a field's face where
tinfoil the landlord hung flashed out
against crows, a sound like far swords.
The robins worked, humorless legions
of fathers, mothers, barely lifting
themselves from shadow to shadow and I

found the pinto mare with the half-born
foal: its black, dirt-clotted nostrils,
the short-haired head all night bobbing,
unable to bring its body forth. I thought
Christ, the son of a bitch landlord again,
asleep, drunk, his unattended toys blown
into death, drifting off without a sound.

Across the pasture the stud's big head
pumped up and down, broad ass scratching
a post as he watched us. Gimpy himself,

he turned away, trotted to deeper green,
one muzzle-muffled snort smart in the air.
Rage? What could he do, or me, or you?
Phantom F-4s from Langley shot overhead.

I wanted to throw rocks, shout, to fist
the sky with anger. Head-down the robins
patiently worked the mud, so I put one
hand on the leathery cheek of the foal
and the other on the pinto's warm rump.
That black eye stuck open, fly-specked,
gleamed when I squatted to look inside.

The past? The future? A small mistake made
in breeding?—I wanted to ask, but the mare
stepped on, head just above the grass-tips,
hunching, trying to eat. Robins waddled in
her smelly wake. I heard her teeth grinding
the small-skull rocks, indifferent to me,
as her spittle cut dirt, chewing the sun.

GARGOYLE

I used to walk that sidewalk in your head
where, in the middle of one block,
the house rose, shabby as a lion out
of the dust, windows glazed with a filth
offering no explanation. Over the door
what must have been a hand's
long-practiced dream appeared every day,
though it had no name, the head
poking itself into the raucous pleasure
along our street, cruising,
its layers of paint like a whore's makeup
shocking, but in the rain sad
as the blank eyes tried to blink it all off.
It was always there, nobody looking,
nobody asking who made this thing,
no answer but the traffic. This was not art,
only the crude moves of thick fingers
that now I think may already be gone from us,
as almost certainly the beast is
cut down who leaped many times in my sleep,
who once hovered in a deep nightmare
I walked into, with a woman dead
and someone skinned-up, weeping.
The people had seen and gathered to watch.
When they walked away, an eye
dark as a window cradled in my hands, but I
threw it from me and saw it shatter.
You could go with me to ask the thick fingers
what it all meant, if we could find them.
But I think even the corrosive smell
of mildew under the house where we lay together
once wouldn't answer. I think
the beast whose body kept hidden in the wall
is only the shape of change, is

gone, the walls are gone, and you and I are
going to walk up our street grown
fully, swaggering, collars open, speaking loud.

From *The Roundhouse Voices* (1985)

THE ROUNDHOUSE VOICES

In full glare of sunlight I came here, man-tall but thin
as a pinstripe, and stood outside the rusted fence
with its crown of iron thorns while
the soot cut into our lungs with tiny diamonds.
I walked through houses with my grain-lovely slugger
from Louisville that my uncle bought and stood
in the sun that made its glove soft on my hand
until I saw my chance to crawl under and get past
anyone who would demand a badge and a name.

The guard hollered I could get the hell from there quick
when I popped in his face like a thief. All I ever wanted
to steal was life and you can't get that easy
in the grind of a railyard. *You can't catch me
Lardass, I can go left or right as good as the Mick,*
I crooned to him, holding my slugger by the neck
for a bunt laid smooth where the coal cars
jerked and let me pass between tracks
until, in a slide on ash, I fell safe and heard
the wheeze of his words: *Who the hell are you, kid?*

I hear them again tonight, Uncle, hard as big brakeshoes,
when I lean over your face in the box of silk. The years
you spent hobbling from room to room alone crawl
up my legs and turn this house to another
house, round and black as defeat, where slugging
comes easy when you whip the gray softball over
the glass diesel globe. Footsteps thump on the stairs
like that fat ball against bricks and when I miss
I hear you warn me to watch the timing, to keep
my eyes on your hand and forget the fence,

hearing also that other voice that keeps me out and away
from you on a day worth playing good ball. Hearing
Who the hell . . . I see myself like a burning speck

of cinder come down the hill and through a tunnel
of porches like stands, running on deep ash,
and I give him the finger, whose face still gleams
clear as a B&O headlight, just to make him get up
and chase me into a dream of scoring at your feet.
At Christmas that guard staggered home sobbing,
the thing in his chest tight as a torque wrench.
In the summer I did not have to run and now

who is the one who dreams of a drink as he leans over
tools you kept bright as a first girl's promise? I
have no one to run from or to, nobody to give
my finger to as I steal his peace. Uncle, the light
bleeds on your gray face like the high barbed-wire
shadows I had to get through and maybe you don't remember
you said to come back, to wait and you'd show me
the right way to take a hard pitch in the sun
that shudders on the ready man. I'm here

though this is a day I did not want to see. In the roundhouse
the rasp and heel-click of compressors is still,
soot lies deep in every greasy fingerprint.
I called you from the pits and you did not come up
and I felt the fear when I stood on the tracks
that are like stars which never lead us
into any kind of light and I don't know who'll
tell me now when the guard sticks his blind snoot
between us: take off and beat the bastard out.
Can you hear him over the yard, grabbing his chest,
cry out, *Who the goddamn hell are you, kid?*

I called him every name in the book, Uncle, but he caught us
and what good did all those hours of coaching do?
You lie on your back, eyeless forever, and I think
how once I climbed to the top of a diesel and stared
into that gray roundhouse glass where, in anger,
you threw up the ball and made a star

to swear at greater than the Mick ever dreamed.
It has been years but now I know what followed
every morning the sun came up, not light
but the puffing bad-bellied light of words.

All day I've held your hand, trying to say back a life,
to get under that fence with words I lined
and linked up and steamed into a cold room
where the illusion of hope means skin torn in boxes
of tools. The footsteps come pounding into words
and even the finger I give death is words
that won't let us be what we wanted, each one
chasing and being chased by dreams in the dark.
Words are all we ever were and they did us
no damn good. Do you hear that?

Do you hear the words that, in oiled gravel, you gave me
when you set my feet in the right stance to swing?
They come coal-hard and they come in wings
and loops like despair not even the Mick
could knock out of this room, words softer
than the centers of hearts in guards or uncles,
words skinned and numbed by too many bricks.
I've had enough of them and bring them back here
where the tick and creak of everything dies
in your tiny starlight and I stand down
on my knees to cry *Who the hell are you, kid?*

HARPERS FERRY

White, slope-shouldered, falling away in shade
as the land falls, windows half-shuttered,
odd glass eyes in the cool morning of fogs.

The seam where each wind will howl is clear,
angles of slats still binding, scarred, the strain
of wood that's warped by bitter winters—who

lived here? we ask, slowing, imagining ourselves
in the cupola tilted like old hope. We stop
and trespass the slant of abandoned floors, steps,

furtive as a family in our talk of what's left.
Here the marriages, divorces, deaths of good wood
remain, mute beginnings, quaint in the snapshots

our children will box up in time: a rotten walk
we took, a tumbled foundation, ancestral hills
that keep heaving up wildflowers, planks, seams.

An Antipastoral Memory
of One Summer

It is written that a single hurricane holds the power
to run our whole country for one year. Imagine
lights in Minnesota chicken coops, firebells
ringing every borough of New York, dock pumps
spewing the bilge from Louisiana shrimpers,
the pulse that sends a voice from San Francisco
to Nagasaki where a woman wakes, folds, and refolds
the American edition of news already forgotten.

Yet even in the dark silos of our countrymen who
practice graceful moves at the missile's panel
(that is like a piano with the amazing, unplayed
notes not even Beethoven could hear into fusion),
no one dreams how to harness the storm for good.
That is why I think of two people at a bulkhead,
an old woman desperately holding down the hem
of her flowered dress, holding a boy's small hand
where the waves they have come to see blossom

one after another, sluicing over their driven hair,
the salt sting so strong their eyes begin to swell,
until they fall back across the elegant Boulevard,
and even there the unexpected crescendos boom in
laces and strings of water radiant as new light.
The noise is unforgettable and deafening, the sea
keeps orchestrating, as if it means to address
all our preparations, the boarded windows, the dead

cars with their rain-blistered glass, the sidewalk
clotted now with seaweed like abandoned bodies.
That suddenly, then, the calm eye stalls on them,
a stillness like a lock with no key, a hand
hovering at a switch, waiting for music unheard,
and see—the woman turns, drags the boy hard

past oaks older than them both, its leaves this fall
blinking like lights, trembling, limbs like spears,
two entering a powerless house to huddle, to pray
to the still God, though they call it hurricane.

THE CHESAPEAKE & OHIO CANAL

Thick now with sludge from years of suburbs, with toys,
fenders, wine bottles, tampons, skeletons of possums,
edged by blankets of leaves, jellied wrappers unshakably
stuck to the scrub pines that somehow lift themselves
from the mossed wall of blockstone headlined a hundred
years back, this water is bruised as a shoe at Goodwill.
Its brown goes nowhere, neither does it remain, and elms
bend over its heavy back like patient fans, dreamlessly.
This is the death of hope's commerce, the death of cities
blank as winter light, the death of people who are gone
erratic and passive as summer's glittering water-skimmers.
Yet those two climbing that path like a single draft horse
saw the heart of the water break open only minutes ago,
and the rainbow trout walked its tail as if the evening
was only an offering in an unimaginable room where planes
inch ahead for the people, as if the trout always meant
to hang from their chain, to be borne through last shades
like a lure drawn carefully, deviously in the blue ache
of air that thickens still streets between brown walls.

GUINEA HENS

They wait where the dirt lane unspools,
round and plump as mock oranges,
almost invisible in the black pines,
their thousands of pinched faces
all turning at once when I come home.
What have I forgotten to be that
my wife should seem in my head
to be waiting among these watchers?
I lean on the wailing motorcycle,
a tide of whiskey unbalancing me,
thinking there may be only one,
her little heels like spurs, a shadow
of her wings floating suddenly past
the shaken headlight I can't control.
This has happened. The night
ought to make me remember things
get tricky on a road like this,
the river's tongue waiting, the red
blink of witnesses who preen, and
the world never helps a bit: it hides
each bump and rut, it flings down
a bird-scream when you least expect
the remembered dead to speak, to heft
the smirking, bottled dark. Lying
beside my love I see how coming home
is the pitched, leaning chance
of flight she fears. Black, sullen,
she screws her grip on this place.
Still, whatever the world says, she's
ready to cackle, crow, rage, strut, be
by morning soft in new light, nibbling.

SKUNKED

Under the womb-heavy wheezing of spruce
she finds him and calls until he slides out,
that big unhousebroken baby we lost.
I watch from an eclipse of floodlights
my wife kneel and try to coax this dog
into a rubber bowl shaped to feed
a sow strong-jawed as death, but he won't
stay, he's racing in the darkness,
stinking up the leaves he goes through.
It's midnight when the sluicing begins,
and her crying. He's still out there
long after the tomato juice has turned
her bath pink as the dawn, after we've
moved two states away, after snow sealed
in whatever expiations we gave ourselves.
Growing to be more than we could handle,
he won't return and we won't return.
We don't have photographs to show us
what happened. But when local dogs
howl like children, when thick summer
leaves us sleepless, oiled with sweat
like breast milk, I hear a snuffling
lift her and draw her out in her gown.
I see the red flow. I hear the spruce
at the first spurts like desire, then
something lets go and we're rooting
in the black yard, calling out names,
boiling water, then waiting as we must,
telling ourselves whatever we have to do
it won't hurt and it won't stink forever.

KITCHEN WINDOWS

Because the house is too small, the season's
feast takes the living room
for its abundant lounge,
a great turkey sliced on the stereo,
bowls of jellied yams, stringbeans, jazzy
stuffing only steps away by plate.
On the table there's chicken,
amber as the last leaves where we park,
and ham singed black,
with toothpicked red ribbons, pineapple
moons like a child's eyes,
a coffee urn with its strong blessing.
Some kneel, some talk. Atop
the television is corn bread, swaddled rolls,
infants of butter, red sauces,
sugar white as snow not here yet, promised.
An old college trunk has preserves
with that odd, eerie sheen
turned bright where television's on,
though no one watches
today's episode, the family soap's hacking
through the holiday fare
of sickness, betrayal, defeat, and the usual
edge of hope they leave
with the grade B cleanser's scum rinsed shiny.
Somewhere there's three
kingly decanters of wine, all domestic.
I walk back through these
rooms to praise what happens to us all,
heaped meals we juggle on knees,
childish as clowns, boffo tales
we tell each on another, breaking into song,
loosening our collared,
formal loves, shifting from wine
to harder things, arms flung now to anyone

suddenly there like an oak
still golden in a world slipped graveyard gray.
How is it we always wind up
in the kitchen, hammy hips on stainless steel,
cheeks booze-ruddy again
that winter will wash pale, smoke hanging
like youth layer on layer,
our butts sizzling out in the sink? I stop
here, coat off, sleeves up,
tight as a tick in the warmth of friends,
laughing, chilled by sweat
on my neck. Soon I will slide out the side
door and stand in the blue
breathhook of nightfall, that sorrow come back
to be forgiven again.
I step to the cool edge of stones at the alley,
not myself, but some other
spirit, benign, from a far wood, and stand
lit up, glowing inside
that long, cast-out hope of kitchen light,
as Chaucer, leaving court,
stood before a gorged family tavern to think
the night enormous and bitter
for so many, yet shadows
already danced, ludicrously brave, and so happy.

From *Gray Soldiers* (1984)

Night Traffic near Winchester, Virginia

From Cumberland's funerals, eldest son, I
lead my survivors south, toward the sea,
past tall ash, through stunning cidery
winesaps still bobbing the Blue Ridge,
the leaf-littered fieldstone walls
drooping like rebel stragglers away
from weathered barns, veterans leaning
quaint as postcards from the dark
Tomb of the Confederate Dead, never
closed, catching the trucks' roar
at Winchester where my father always
stopped to eat. Here, we descend

into the Valley, slow to a stop-and-go,
crawl through painted brick cottages
huddled at sidewalks like history,
heartpine floors sloped so badly
water runs off before it stains.
Like the hips of ancestors, each
foundation is cracked and patched,
the windows narrow as eyes, crusty
along the once horse-clotted street.
Tourists find here the cheery, yellow
farmhouse used by Stonewall Jackson
to plot cavalry raids thunderous
as the black Bible he slept with.
It's dark as a mapcase now, closed.

I promise kids we'll stop another time,
long enough to see boots, old orders,
the grim portraits staring at war,
but now we climb, car straining, up
the dark's deadly ridge, and halt
before our drop to the plains. Here

my father stopped with me, heading
north to bury the fallen kin. Stepping
out, I feel the chill, rare night drift
me back to the smell of his coffee.

This is the way to grandmother's, he'd say,
pointing into the sky, so I say it,
on the cliff, no grandmother left, and
behind us nothing's changed, motors
howl all night, voices that roar
as teamsters did, hearing the rumor—
"Grant's taken Charlottesville,"
but tonight just the march of boys
looking for girls, trucks for home.
It's only Route 17, the country way.

But my son, old as I was with my father,
climbs over our girls sleeping, steps
to the overlook's lipfall I don't
need to look at, the historical blank
that never stops falling here. Still,
I come behind him, take his hand.
His athletic jacket shines like cities
at Christmas, its faint galaxies
of light shifting as the body moves.
Out there we see the neon welcome
of blue Sears, Kmart red, streets
steady with taillights like campfires.

When once I asked my father which army
was here those long nights, he said
We were men, just going up and down.
Afraid, he said, glad for a fire.
Our fathers and fathers of fathers.
In the cold of mountains I'm afraid
at this edge and feel the hand asking
"How far have we come?" I could say

I don't know, the usual evasion,
but over the lights, the dotted road,
I hear an old voice I had thought lost
say *Far, but not far enough yet.*
Ahead, our family will stand awake,
lights on, coffee hot, ready for news.

PHOTOGRAPH OF A CONFEDERATE SOLDIER STANDING ON ROCKS IN THE JAMES RIVER AT RICHMOND

                                        A light rises,
falls, floats around the frame, a kind
of water swirling through generations
of years, pooling and shining when we look
at oblique corners, a given-back glimmer of one
come from a thatch of hickory heaving the home-field
still in his head, this boy turned in the sun's
stunned spilling where the river is
bristly as bayonets rippling, one
hung in light like a leaf above lipping dark,
the hem of his greatcoat outflung.

                                        Why is he there? What man
in the war's middle stands like this with the teeth-
ragged remains of Richmond looming to the north?
We think he may dream of days the acorns
shelled down through yellow leafburst,
or mother's hand on him because in pools
the brackish bluegills would not
let him go home on time. Why
do we not think of a throat's thick fear?
Can fear be that shining on his face? Maybe

                                        Fall's glory
that must be in each thread of the sorry homespun
he has taken through a toil of sun somehow
lets loose, leaves him alone. All his life
he remembers this walk, this stone-cradle turning
his face up to cliffs. We can almost see him think
not once can he say why he came, nor give any answer
for what in this split second nails him forever
as no bullet could.

                    Expressionless, he seeks us,
one-eyed, an eyepatch rampant over the left shoulder,
the right eye dark as a wound, and he cannot see
all the light in the world holds us to him,
all we are, the uncreated future,
                                    the image
which begins here as one apprehension
in the nerves of men, the secret
bond we almost know in that
instant we turn and lift ourselves
from the black river-roar and light-swarm.

IRONCLAD

I'm ten, spending the summer with my grandmother,
let loose, wandering the mossed bulkhead
where the tide swings too far in
to walk the little sand of Hampton Roads.

I sit in the grass under the steel historical sign
that says if I look a hundred blue years out
I'll see that battle of the first Ironclads,
three hours of clanging and no decision,

no casualties until at noon the Monitor's cheesebox
hull shudders, its sight hole flares wide,
blinding the skipper, Lieutenant Worden.
I think of those seamen, speechless in chugging blue

where a peach in my hand is soft as a skull, one side
going red with the dusk while the Purple Martins
swoop, sleek shadows, so close I hear
the wingbeats like distant hearts. But I don't

eat, I don't move when my name steams out of the dark.
How can I when I haven't seen the battle end,
those iron tubs fighting like twins, night
already pushing them back in the wind? Off Hatteras

one day I'll see my squad of divers cast a net of light
over sand holding the Monitor like a woman asleep.
What brings the storm, moves the ship, hides
still its crew's heartbeat in cold blue

tons of water until the radar shows it rising clear
as a tumor on florescent screens? None of us knows
enough to resurrect this ghost. Sonar's ping
reports odd calling sounds, probably weather, but

turned blue and gray by the television's newscast
on this Atlantic night, I remember my grandmother
promised to find me in storms, and did. Her face
feathers near, calls past machines that pump, is

gone where the hospital room's iron surf beats on.
I was ten, held by eerie squadrons of killdeer.
Oh sailors of the dark, I want your whistle
to haul me aboard. I want to hear you call forever.

LEAFLESS TREES, CHICKAHOMINY SWAMP

Humorless, hundreds of trunks, gray in the blue expanse
where dusk leaves them hacked like a breastwork,
stripped like pikes planted to impale, the knots
of vines at each groin appearing placed by makers
schooled in grotesque campaigns. Mathew Brady's
plates show them as they are, the ageless stumps,
timed-sanded solitaries, some clumped in squads
we might imagine veterans, except they're only wood,
and nothing in the world seems more dead than these.

Stopped by the lanes filled with homebound taillights,
we haven't seen the rumored Eagle we hoped to watch,
only a clutch of buzzards ferrying sticks for a nest.
Is this history, that we want the unchanged, useless
spines out there to thrust in our faces the human
qualities we covet? We read this place like generals
whose promised recruits don't show, who can't press on:
we feel the languor of battle, troops unable to tell
themselves from the enemy, and a file-hard fear gone

indifferent in the mortaring sun that will leave all
night after night standing in the same cold planes
of water. It never blooms or greens. It merely stinks.
Why can't we admit this is death's gift, the scummy
scene of our pride, blown brainpans of a century ago?
Why do we sit and sniff the rank hours inside words
blunt as ground that only stares off our question: what
happened? Leaf-light in our heads, don't we mean why
these grisly emblems, the slime that won't swell to hope?

The rapacious odor of swamps all over the earth bubbles
sometimes to mist, fetid flesh we can't see but know,
just cells composing, decomposing, a heart's illusions.
God knows what we'd do in there, we say, easing back
on the blacktop. Once we heard a whistling. Harmonicas?

But who'd listen? Surely all was green once, fragile
as a truce, words braiding sun and water, as on a lake
where families sang. What else would we hope for, do
in the dead miles nothing explains or changes or relieves?

Caravati's Salvage: Richmond

He's the reaper, the buyer, the keeper of grand houses
gone to pieces, and the choice parts are here.
You want big doors, brass knobs, stained glass?
A hand-carved box? Grandfather clocks, a chandelier?

Maybe those shutters that lined Monument Avenue,
heartwood, the paint age-blistered, kept closed
a decade, some of them, when Lee died? Or you
desire staircase, railing, marble mantels, bellows—

he's stacked it all in heaps high as a pile of guns.
Ask. Caravati keeps. Endless old names, how they lived.
Eighty-three, hair white as nightgowns in the sun,
he'll guide you, touching each piece, a man you'd give

a fortune to, in his foyer, summoned by his bell,
for the secrets you covet. He stands still as delight.
He offers water, a beaded jar, from his old well.
The one his fathers dug. Way down, cold, sweet.

From *In the House of the Judge* (1983)

PHOTOGRAPHIC PLATE, PARTLY SPIDERED, HAMPTON ROADS, VIRGINIA, WITH MODEL T FORD MID-CHANNEL

No one alive has seen such ice but the five-mile floor
of water so clenched itself salt broke down.
Among us even the age-wearied would not dream
you might walk the Chesapeake Bay
and look unafraid on its lucid darkness,

and the fathers of fathers, boatwrights, sailors of all
waters, never guessed this stuttering machine
might take them so far. But someone,
joking maybe, rolled that small house
on perilous wheels down the banks
of the James, gunned it forward
for skids, runs, circles, a day
of such joyous noise the dead
seemed to have risen, so many
great-booted and black-coated are out there.

We cannot tell what they think, who find themselves
dancing on the road where no road ever was,
out there with the long skirts, a few
thick-waisted grandmothers, even
a scatter of children cast about.
All of them face east to Norfolk
where ships doze like the unimaginable
beasts the sea has given to men's dreams.

The Model T is small, black, plain, and appears
cornered like something risen through ice.
Hands reach in the hazed air
but do not touch what must be
chugging in a kind of terror.
The plate is dotted far and near.
Seagulls? Stains? Some mistake of glass?
Why do their faces look down, as if averted?

Among these is the one who will breed us, having crossed
a whiteness he will not speak about even to her
whose skirts he will shake us from.
But now gears spin inside him,
wheels, a future of machines. One day
he will tell my father he walked on water . . .
sick, chugging for breath, shunned as crazy,
who I remember by the habitual odor of gasoline.
When he died my father said he was too frightened to live.

Under the ice where they walk the dark is enormous.
All day I watch the backs turned away
for the one face that is mine,
that is going to wheel at me the secrets of many.

Of Oystermen, Workboats

The wide, white, wing-boned washboards of twenty
footers, sloped, ridged to hold
a man's tongs and stride,

                    the good stance
to scrape deep with a motion like big applause,
plunging the teeth true beyond the known
mounds of the dead, the current carried
cloisters of murk,
                 miracles that bloom
luminous and unseen, sweet things to be
brought up, bejeweled, culled from husks,

as oystermen like odd angels glide far off enough
to keep a wake gentle as shirts on a line,
red baseball caps dipping like bloodied
heads upright, the clawed hands slapped
at the air in salute,
                     those washboards that splinter
the sun on tongs downlaid, on tines humming,

those womb-hulls harbored flank to flank at dusk
until the white-robed priest of the moon
stands tall to the sea's spume-pour
in nostrils
              of the men who sway from heel to heel,

the season come again, the socketed gray
of their eyes rolling outward,
forearms naked past longjohns,
the salted breast-beaters at first light

lined up, ready to fly.

SMITHFIELD HAM

Aged, bittersweet, in salt crusted, the pink meat
lined with the sun's flare, fissured.
I see far back the flesh fall
as the honed knife goes
through the plate, the lost
voice saying ". . . it cuts easy as butter. . . ."

Brown sugar and grease tries to hold itself
still beneath the sawed knee's white.
Around the table the clatter of china
kept in the highboy echoes,
children squeal in a near room.

The hand sawing is grandfather's, knuckled,
steadily starting each naked plate
heaped when it ends. Mine
waits shyly to receive
under the tall ceiling
all the aunts, uncles have gathered to hold.

My shirt white as the creased linen, I shine
before the wedge of cherry pie, coffee
black as the sugarless future.
My mother, proud in his glance,
whispers he has called for me and for ham.

Tonight I come back to eat in that house the sliced
muscle that fills me with an old thirst.
With each swallow, unslaked, I feel
his hand fall more upon mine,
that odd endless blessing
I cannot say the name of . . .
the dead recalled, the jobless
with low sobs, sickness, the Depression.

Chewing, I ask how he is. Close your mouth, she says.
This time, if he saw me, maybe he'd remember
himself, who thanklessly carved us
the cured meat. The Home holds
him in darkness like coffee
we poured those days. I gnaw
a roll left too long, dried hard.

When my knife drags across the plate,
my mother shakes her head, whining like a child.
Nothing's sharp anymore, I can't help it, she says.
Almost alone, I lift the scalded coffee.
My mouth, as if incontinent,
dribbles and surprises us.

Her face is streaked with summer
dusk where katydids drill and die out.
Wanting to tell her there's always tomorrow,
I say "You're sunburned. Beautiful as ever."
Gardening puts the smell of dirt on her.
Like a blade, her hand touches mine.

"More?" Then, "You'll never get
enough, you think, so sweet,
until the swelling starts,
the ache, the thirst that wants
to bust a person open late at night."
I fill my cup again, drink, nod, and listen.

SNAPSHOT OF A CRAB-PICKER, AMONG BARRELS SPILLING OVER, APPARENTLY AT THE END OF HER SHIFT

Clacking and gouging when huddled,
these well-armed warriors
sweat in dimmed sun and scuttle
in the small space each has.
Long arms salute liegelords just
passed, shadows, the honed meat
hard under those scarred helmets.
Sea promised they come and wait,
season and season always the same.

Near these the squat houses, lights
burled, where a girl will go step
athwart the sharp road of shells
down to a shadow who's dug in
his feathery heels and hovers now
as the liquid night swells, lifts
her with first mooncrest to ride
upon him until she will lie
pale in the frost's breath, spent
flesh the white flaky treasure
these homebound, wordless, breed.

What they offer she will offer,
with sea-smell on her hands
that clean and cradle and keep
against the dull day hours
of simple dreams: hunger, flight,
the tidal force like despair
that under moons shall idle,
singing for the armorless one
love she smiles at, a taste,
faint, she cannot flee ever,
of legions around her biting.

BATS

Still in sleeping bags, the promised delivery
only words as usual, our lives upside down,
we are transients lost in thirteen rooms
built by a judge who died. The landlord says
they mean no harm, the bats, and still I wake
at the shrill whistling, the flutter overhead.

I fumble to a tall window open among maples.
A car crawling a hill splashes my face with light
spread fine by mist that had been summer rain,
a sweetness that drips from black-palmed leaves.
The breeze I feel is fresh, edged with mown hay,

enough to make me think the thumps and titters
I hear might be the loving pleasure of parents
unguessed, a long quarrel ended, a thrilling
touch that trails to muffled play. But these
are bats, shadows, residents of the house elders
built to last, the vaulted attic tall as a man

holding them hung in rows daylong like words
unuttered above the yard where children romp.
Flashlight in hand, I pass through the parlor
papered in silk for marriages the judge made,
and stand beneath the hidden door. The truth is

nothing can drive them out or contravene those
fretful, homespinning voices we cannot help
fearing as if they were the all-knowing dead.
Yet if I had one chair to stand tall enough on
I would climb with my light and shaking voice
to see whatever has lodged in their wizened eyes.

Under a room I have never seen but know, I stand
like one of the unblessed at the edge of dawn.

Smelling mold, I hear a dog's hopeless howl
and think of the stillness in the deep heads
of those who hang in sleep that may be like love

in the children we cannot keep forever as they are.
Each one near me is furled in a homeholding song no
darkness or deed can kill. With them all dreams
bring the fields' fresh life here to hum over.
As if I had never been out of this room, I listen.
The sound is like rain, leaves, or sheets settling.

Turn-of-the-Century House

The leaded, wiggly glass lives in its human length
as the squall, unpredicted, slams me down late
at night to see what in the world goes on wailing.
We have no lights. Lightning like a girl's grin
stands me dead center of the parlor. It's maples.

This house has its jitters yet. It's unreconstructed,
two claw-footed bathtubs, taps that won't turn off,
doors refusing their frames. Often they danced here.
Stars on the tin roof marked the place from near hills,

settling thick as a shawl on a woman shaken awake.
It was only memory, but she woke her sisters anyway.
They stood on linoleum. Glass rattled and pipes clanged.
A bad storm, couldn't they see that? Ice, then snow.

The maples no one could bear cutting down, dangerous now,
raked the roof. Stars turned to ice, blinding the glass.
Can you see them, trying to sing as you would? Cold
swirls at the feet, dull yellow, naked as planked maple.
Water in the pipes forms red-streaked and pearl nails.

HOUSE MOVERS

Steadily down highways intractable roofs creep.
Whoever chooses them seems of one mind.
Sad white, pale green, the imagined result
of a going-out-of-business operation,
their clapboard hulls betray storied weather
by flaking paint and those stone-cracked
glasses just violated. Behind them steps
hang patiently, or a family porch waits
like a quick amazed countryman. Required,
we think, are brute shoulders, blue jaws
and knuckles that gently graze a child's
face sliding under the edge of sleep.
These do not go with the houses, moored
families who seem alive only near pastures
where their fathers have lain for years.
Empty of each worn table and broken chair
used long nights to conjure, talk, puzzle,
the houses glide over our roads like veins,
ominous as we pass them and grip our wheels.
Wherever they arrive hard ground is gouged,
papers solemnly signed, lime is laid out,
the gray, bony bite of foundations readied.
We imagine, driving sometimes behind them,
the black birdwings will start up, spiral,
a furred knob in the sumac will shudder,
clench itself down, and growl in its belly.
In a week no one will stop to feel suddenness
hunch unalterably there, like a growth,
or months after will remember what was
never so stingingly white. But shouldered
quietly at that rutted ground, our children
those first hours wait for children to pop out.
They lick their lips at the future come
as unlikely as death or birth among them.
Here, too, arrive the unsummoned about us,

from the tree-shrouded edges we live near,
the thick-thighed ones who pull and strike,
wielders of maul and nail and cold chain.
When we step in their tracks we become
the bare-soled children of their keeping.
We dance out of their way, transfixed.
At night, our houses locked, we cannot guess
who chose how we would lie under all this.
In our heads their walls ring, bow, and chant.

IN THE HOUSE OF THE JUDGE

All of them asleep, the suspiring everywhere is audible weight
  in the winter-shadowed house where I have dreamed
      night after night and stand now trying
  to believe it is only dust, no more than vent-spew
      risen from the idiotically huffing
grandfather of a furnace in the coal room's heart of darkness.

Haven't I touched the flesh-gray sift on bookshelves, on framed
      dim photographs of ancestors, on clotted arms
  of the banjo clock that tolls past
    all resemblance to time, clicking like a musket's
steel hammer? And every day I wipe my glasses but still it comes,
     as now, at the top of the whining stairs, I am

come to wait with my hand laid light on the moon-slicked railing.
  I hear the house-heave of sleepers, and go jittery
    with no fear I can name. I feel myself
  shaped by the mica-fine motes that once were one
    body in earth until gouged, cracked,
left tumbled apart and scarcely glowing in a draft-fanned pit.

Pipes clank and gargle like years in the ashen veins of the Judge.
    They came to his house, the dung-heeled, some
    drunk, all with stuttered pleas to free
      their young, who could make it given a chance, just
one more good chance, so they said. Impassive, skin-folds thick
   as a lizard, he stared at the great one for a sign, that

dog across the room, who kept a wary eye and was a one-man dog.
  Overhead do the same unbearable stars yet wheel
     in bright, ubiquitous malice, and what
  am I, wiping my glasses, certain this house walks
    in nail-clicking threat, going to plead?
I look out through warped Civil War glass buffed by men now ash

where the small park he gave in civic pride lies snow-blistered.
Subzero then, as now, sent fire in the opening
throat, but they came: tethered horses,
striding shadows, women who shrieked nightlong
until even gone they continued in his head. He heard breathing.
He painted his house perfectly white.

I stare at that snow as at a scaffold. Whose lightening footprints
could soften my fear or say why I sniff like a
dog, seem to taste a skim of black air
upsweeping the maple stairwell, and feel my hair
go slowly white? How many hours must
a man watch snow shift the world before he sees it is only a dream

of useless hope stamped and restamped by the ash-steps of those we
can do no justice to but in loving them? But
what could he do before the raw facts
of men cleaving flesh like boys hacking ice?
I think how he must have thought of his barking teacher of law:
There is only truth and law! He had learned the law.

But what was the truth to leave him trembling, a child in prayer?
In late years he kept the monster by his side, two shades
walking alone in the ice, the nail-raker, one
who howled without reason and clawed at the heart
of door after door. In the end he was known
inseparable from his beast who, it was said, kept the Judge alive.

Until he was not. Until his house emptied. Until we came who I
hear
breathing, heads warm as banked ash at my hand
laid light as I have laid it on this railing.
But are we only upfloating and self-clinging ash
that loops freely through dark houses? Those enigmatic fissures
I see circling the snow—are those only the tracks

of the dog I locked out, those black steps no more than a gleaming
  ice, or the face of some brother in the dirt betrayed,
    pleading, accusing? The moon, far off and dim,
  plays tricks with my eyes and the snow path turns dark as
a line of men marched into the earth. Whitely, my breath floats
    back at me, crying *I did not do this,* when the shuddering

courthouse clock across the square booms me back. Dream's
      aftershock, the heirloom banjo starts to thud, drum,
  so I turn and hustle downstairs to halt it.
      Even with my hands on its hands it wants to thump
its malicious heart out, but I can do this at least: I can hold on
    to help them sleep through another night. For all

I can sit for a while with love's ice-flickering darkness where ash
  is heavily filling my house. I can sit with my own
    nailed walker in the snow, one whistled
  under my hand without question or answer. If I sleep
he will pad the floors above the fire-pit. He will claw me awake
    to hear breathing in the still house of the Judge

      where I live.

From *Homage to Edgar Allan Poe* (1981)

DESKS

Piled on a loading dock where I walked,
  student desks battered, staggered
by the dozens, as if all our talk
  of knowledge was over,

as if there'd be no more thin blondes
  with pigtails, no math, no art,
no birds to stare at. Surplus now, those molds
  we tried to sleep in, always hard

so it wouldn't be pleasant and we'd fall
  awake in time for the one question
with no answer. Quiet as a study hall,
  this big place, this final destination,

oblivious to whatever the weather is,
  hearing the creak of the wind's weight.
The desks are leg-naked, empty, as if
  we might yet come, breathless, late.

And all that time I thought of the flames
  I hadn't guessed, of one
I had loved for years, how the names
  carved one into another would

all scar out the same, blunt, in blue
  searing, like love's first pain.
I stood there like a child, scared, new,
  bird-eyed, not knowing why I came.

POND

The soft forgiving ooze of the pond's bottom,
that cool fluid move through the toes
when you step out just beyond roots,
through weeds, into that black slough

that the dream has warned is love's terror:
to stand in this abiding rut among shells
born of ancestors, bearing the future,
is to feel all the flesh in the world

and to think of the last time you were in love,
the vertigo, the skidding infinite sky,
the lily's perfect, opening moves,
that slippery reek, that quick eternity.

HOMAGE TO EDGAR ALLAN POE

The Hygeia Hotel

When I was six grandparents brought me here in a Hudson
green as the swamps of the Chesapeake.

We passed through the gates of Fort Monroe to the seawall.
With string and a fresh chicken neck
I tried for the great Blue Crab.

They walked the promenade before the towering hotel.
Their war was over.
Now and then I might see them
gathered in knots, men in strange brown suits,
women holding pastel skirts that bloomed in the wind.

Like flowers they swayed, smudged with tears.
That was 1948. I was impatient to go.
Once, holding hands, we went up the wide gray stairs.

Waiters scurried, white silk shirts, black pants.
Through tight lips they spoke softly.
The candles held all dim,
as if the war kept on.

Later, we watched the Bay Line's steamer *Pocahontas*
glide away north to Baltimore.

Tonight steamed crabs are in the air and the moon
and mud's black flesh come forth at low tide.
Here, in 1849, Miss Ingram of Norfolk
heard Poe read "Ulalume."

In three days he would die screaming on a table,
the poet possessed by the slosh and slime
of America. She wrote:

"There were many persons on the long verandas
that surrounded the hotel, but they seemed
remote and far away."

In the Hudson going home that night, I was buried
between the old ones, their bodies ripe.
Around us night congealed.

Ahead, the steady toss of the Chesapeake. Headlights
clawed the dark. I was too small to see much,
frightened by the voice on the radio
declaiming "The Shadow Knows."

Nekkid

          Why was I there?
Fourteen, lank, moody, marked
by appetites that seeped up like convictions
in parents, shipped to summer camp near Richmond,

I wasn't Robbie or Bill, his drowned brother.
I would not launch myself stark *nekkid*
from the sycamore, however summer blistered,
however girls in canoes cheered,
however welcome might be the hole
of the James River.

I sucked in my Poe, suffered, at near anything flared,
thus was let alone, as weird.

Wearing black jeans, T-shirt, boots, I climbed beyond
a ragtop Ford parked, past an old wooden bridge
plodded in my sweat along a path
that took me one morning clear

to a humped outcrop of bare stone with a view
of the valley, the river, and Poe's city.

                                        Below,
curves, mounds, swelling distances straight down.
I edged out by inches, as if to the lip of truth,
daring death or fate, and stripped to my chest
and shouted at the depths.
Unanswered, I backed up, afraid of the fall,

but saw Richmond erect over its cobblestoned streets.
From windows slaves framed in the air
the sun piked back
out of warehouses and wharves,
the prison, taverns, the sleeping rooms of whores,

so I imagined. Easy to believe Poe came from this.
In my mind a manly city, state, what I wanted,
not my maze of green, long days with guides
droning the names of leaves.
What did I know of sap rising in veined hollows?

I climbed because I wanted to *see*,
and not just the close-lapping slit
of the river you wallow in and never know.
I wanted to look at the whole spread-eagled beauty,
the thick pollution of foam
spit along the pink bumps and archipelagos.
I knew that down there the boys went nekkid
and I would sometime, maybe.
                                        Robbie's brother
told me it would be like swimming to the bottom,
your toes pushing from that muck,
eyes closed, trying to feel
your way headfirst to the air.
Then you'd scream. And you'd stink.

Climbing down with hunger to those I'd left bobbing
slick in the shallow pools, somewhere
from a socket of leaves

I heard it—
                    that scoring wheeze of the flesh.
I stopped, uncertain, shadowed, still
hearing Robbie's brother's
imitation, maybe.

Her legs waved naked across his back.
As pale as I was, he buried himself in her
while I watched her face roll toward me and wink.
She grinned, whispered, while he plunged, near
enough I seemed to *feel* his shout:

                    "You son of a bitch!"

I ran certain this meant my throat cut,
busting through bush, my body ripping vines loose
that brought blood, and wasn't caught.
Unless you count nights lying awake, shaken, hoping
each rumor of footstep or leaf-fall meant
she had come to call me into darkness.

Unless you count that appalling, grinning face
I carted home the summer I passed through Richmond.
Unless you count the wishing I was not
weird, not in love with her wink,
and not a son of a bitch
to be flung like spit into the universe.

132

Nightcrawlers

I thought of an old crabber, a figure draining his bottle,
tossing it as he trolled in toward the pier
lit up yellow, late, lonely.

His hands tying down the 24-foot scow would seem to glow,
(as if he was holy flesh, I almost wrote)
black crabs bubbling in the barrel.

Under stars glowing like a small town sitting to supper,
I took off my shoes and walked again. Was he
invented, scowling, raw-faced?

Deep black summer grass, and wet, took me through sandyards
where people coaxed roses, and crawlers lugged.
Squashed as I stepped. *Phrenologists call it*

veneration, Poe wrote. I stood near the wharf's bobbing,
shunting hulls for whoever might come. Water,
gasoline slicked, seemed alive with worms.

In my poems I had made him hard-shelled, possessed,
like Edgarpoe, battler with seas, mystic eye.
This one was fat and clumsy

as he wedged the deadrise hull to its slip, pots, tools,
crabs sent atumble, shuddering, the rest flung
down the gullet of her wheelhouse.

No word between us heroic or miserable. It passed,
that grunt of a face going home, sneakers
squishing as he hefted his catch.

As regards the greater truths, men oftener err by
seeking them at the bottom than at the top.
Can the imagination lie? Then, what good?

All I found was this local genius, the tired
heave of him dark as flounder eyes
where the kitchen table was set.

She put the crab meat white as swan feathers before him.
His platter steamed under the grace he spoke.
I thought of Poe, womanless, wormy.

She kissed lightly the old one's salted neck, and sank
beside him while he ate, both
exhausted, luminous.

A Dream of Poe in New York

Worked over here, I'm screwed.
I leave the bar, walk, a man
in need of a woman. She who's
what I deserve is no bargain.

Losing her smell's the problem.
Her light touch turns greasy.
The street glistens like phlegm.
Then rain's spurt plummeting.

Unwashed, wet, I'm left ever
filthier, shaking with it.
An X-rated theater's
screen swallows me with tits,

until I flash Helen, above
all the dark staired and steep,
naked, waiting. Don't love
and flesh differ? Flesh reeks.

The light here's never good.
It blinds like history, twists
truth obscenely, boils blood,
makes you drool, worse, beshit

in Baltimore, as I was once.
I can't forget their pleas,
women with quick hands, tongues.
They turn to scabs. But she,

my late, untouched one, renews
me when I dream, her rivet
of nerves, her lips, the brute
bed-dent we'll make. Her breasts

shine through these visual aids,
redeeming Poe, sot and poet.
My cousin Tate says I'm dead.
White blood flecks her slack lips.

And what is that? say you.
Keep innocent, America—
Death is our great virtue.
Purer than sex, it's perfect.

Yet who in bed or tomb
wants that? *Can you pay, honey?*
I want to be human.
Whatever. You pay, you play.

The End of Everything

How it glints out where least expected, the pink
spread of dawn light in clots of ice

where the milk-horse of the past always broke through
night's crust. I have risen with air in my throat

blooming, shouldering up its white stalk. My love, lying
behind me in a fragrant bed, remarks how precious

is "the shining body of the world." And there, greasy,
over the windowsill, the mushrooming first light

(red as bougainvillaea) silently crawls the naked street
where the horse once stood huffing, nearly invisible,

its spine enough to shatter starlight, a jeweler's blade
cracking loose a final fire. Look at it running

in the wheel's ruts, a pulse intermittent, ectoplasmic.
Like the wings of Pegasus beating themselves to dust.

Now on elbows, keeping my nightmarish face outside
the room where she stirs to silk, I speak of the great

pink-orange orchid of the future, serenely, soundlessly
sucking our breath to its bloom above the manure piles.

Steamer to Baltimore

Tonight you and I watch stars at the bow,
our heads draped over, giddy with blood,
body and boat drifting the same sky he saw.
Poe, the American, once rode Chesapeake
channels inward in wind-fret where seahawks
blinked like critics in cordgrass. He believed
always in the perfect gaze of love that waits
beyond the ebb and crest of time. The moon
we ride on breaks for this rib-thudding scow
to go where his dream flowed. Many of us
line the rail, faces the tide floats apart,
each one Edgarpoe, unknown, going home.
Whisker clouds swirl east leaving Baltimore
as engines churn, the raked hull digs and broods.

Wedding Song

Camden, North Carolina, is not picturesque
though it is the place we remember
where many men and women have gone
in good luck and bad to repair
aching hearts: for five dollars
no one asks your age or looks for the curve

swelling under the skirt of the cheerleader.
Our justice of the peace pumped gas
and spoke the words through gums
long toothless and tobacco black.
A tourist honked for help.

He gave each of us a sample box of Cheer.
Y'all come on back anytime!

The first time down Route 17, by George Washington's
ditch, he of the chopped cherries,
we turned back in the Dismal Swamp.
Who could make up a truer thing than that?

You weren't fooling. Neither was I.
The second time we made it.

A wheezing clerk above an X-rated movie house
slowly printed our names.
He chewed an onion's golden rings.
He said *Are you now or have you ever been crazy?*

Weren't we? Isn't love something that breaks,
drooling and dangling inside
like a car's hot-water hose
that leaves you helpless,
godforsaken in the middle of nowhere?

Y'all come on back anytime.
Fifty bucks and two economy boxes of Cheer—
how far could we get on that?

I was certain you'd end up croaking home
to mother after those early months.

Our first house had more holes
than we could cover, mice,
snakes, spiders, our dinner guests.

In that place you woke to the screams of a mare
who dropped half of her foal, dragging
half around the rented house until
with tractor and chain
the landlord delivered us.

The chain still dangles in your dreams,
and his *Y'all come on back anytime!*

Sometimes when I think we have learned
to live in the world, the faces
of children lining our walls,
the darkness waiting ahead
like a swamp that's no joke,

I turn and find you coiled in a corner of light.
I think of the five green dollars unfurled
for that clerk of hunger and fools,
the blue acrid soap
that scoured us cherry red,
and the screams of our years.

Are we now or were we ever crazy?
Sign here, the man said, and we did,
the voices of men and women

making love, cracking up
through that black movie floor.

I hear them still.

for Dee

READING THE BOOKS
OUR CHILDREN HAVE WRITTEN

They come into the room while quail are crying to huddle up,
canyon winds just beginning. They pass my big brown desk,
faces damp and glistening as freshly washed peaches,
and offer themselves to be kissed. Everything's father,
I kiss them, I say *See you tomorrow!* Their light steps
fade down stairs, what they are saying like the far stars
shrill, hard to understand. They try to say how a father
writes his book, how they are in it, who are his loves.
Then in their beds they wait for sleep, sometimes singing.

Later I get up and go down in darkness to find the hour
before they were scrubbed, before they brought me new faces.
There on the floor I find stapled pages, the mild, strange
countenances of animals no one has ever seen, the tall man
who writes an endless story of those homeless in the night.
They have numbered each page and named each colorful wing.
They have done this to surprise me, surprising themselves.
On the last yellow page one has written: *This is a poem!*
Under this the other one's crayon answers: *See tomorrow!*

From *Dream Flights* (1981)

ELEGY IN AN ABANDONED BOATYARD

> *. . . mindful of the unhonored dead*
> —Thomas Gray

Here they stood, whom the Kecoughtan first believed
gods from another world, one pair of longjohns
each, bad-yellow, knotted with lice,
the godless, bandy-legged runts
with ear bit off, or eye gouged,
$\qquad\qquad\qquad$ who killed and prayed
over whatever flew, squatted, or swam.

In huts hacked from mulberry, pine, and swamp cyprus,
they huddled ripe as hounds.
At cockcrow scratched, shuffled marsh paths,
took skiffs and ferried to dead-rise scows,
twenty-footers dutifully designed and of right draft
for oysters, crabs, and croakers.
$\qquad\qquad\qquad$ They were seaworthy.

According to diaries hand-scrawled, and terse court records,
our ancestors: barbarous, habitual, Virginians.

Some would not sail, came ashore, walked on the land,
kept faces clenched, lay seed and family,
moved often, and are gone. Of them
this harbor says nothing.
Of the sea's workmen, not much,
no brass plate of honor, no monument in the square,
no square, merely the wreckage of a place.

$\qquad\qquad\qquad$ But they stood—
proud, black and white, surly in mist
at the hovel of the boatwright, arm pointed:

Build me one like that yonder!
Meaning the gray hull I see across a cove,
bottom up, canting, nameless now as the hard,
long arm, daddy's or granddaddy's, that points, but
known to the one said to crush clams in his palms, thus
got paid, always, who built the derelicts, and who,
barring feud, took stick in hand here, made
that grave gouged line of a keel,

                    then his broad brow

lifted seaward, in silence, sometimes
summoning a shape in memory, and it hove up, and was
changed some, they whined, but God knows
all they wanted, all he made for them was
to be a little unlike the drab hulls
of the dead ones, but not too much.
                              Like that one yonder!

This was the image he gave them to dream of change,
tomorrow only a guess, the sea's story their
life-stink and bow-slam and stillness, and they
saw how the fair ones grew, quick riddle-riders
our fathers feared, schools that gave us
a message sewn on chest, Bible, slate,
and this worm-holed future entered

blindly as I now have entered his place, feeling
for log-char, back-flung gates of light,
and the builder.
                    Like that one . . .
the lies begin, each inventing why
he should rise up, he should hack out
the joy they dream, his pitch boiled, black
as mud seaming their legs.

Suddenly, I see
and take up a cap left as worthless on a stump, its
stained round fitting my head like water.

Merely to wait where the builder heaved shards and chips
and abortive clots to the tide's tongue-lap
is to feel the unconceived shape pulse
down his arm, into fingers
that took up that stick to let loose
the ingathered wilderness
of dreams: loon, crow, osprey, gull, the man
who cannot believe what he sees, but still sees it.

                              An immense shadow
making over water.

                    Stick in hand, eyes squint. And

                there it is,
                                    the wind cradling

of an Eagle, wing-sails, unfurled, bow-chopping
white water head on, a creature now there, now gone.
A man, I have to hold my face up, study how
air heats, builds a rising push until the high
circle of sight skids out everywhere.

                        Dreaming change,

I understand, almost, the problem: is he not harnessed,
himself, this light flyer, this father
designed to sail like a small god, to screech
down upon pine-huddled, hungry chicks he must
send off with his lethal, air-buoyed shape?
Nothing in him asks what is
        over the wave-edge

                    where our brothers float and sink,
lovely shadows, by the millions.
Putting my back to the sea-worn trunk
they have left me, I pull the stick through
the dirt, and remember the long line,
man-weight in it, and dark-buoyed.

                              It grows
with freckling light, with the answering of birds
crying out the only speech we all have
above our unfinished country
that looms still in the soul,
that would bear us hence,
out of the water that beats in,
out of the water that bore us all here.

The Tire Hangs in the Yard

1

First it was the secret place where I went to dream, end
of the childhood road, deep-tracked, the dark
behind my best friend's house, blackberry
thickets of darkness, and later where
we stared, with willing girls, into the sky.

Past that hedgerow, past fields turned to houses, past
the crows we shot in our bored pleasure, I drive
bathed by green dashlight and the sun's blood
glinting on leaves just parted, then see

again the road's dead-end in woods, its deep stillness
ticking like throat-wheeze—and Jesus Christ
look at the beer cans, the traffic, even
hung on a berry vine somebody's rubber,
and wouldn't you know it that tire still hangs.

2

On the Churchland Baptist Church the hot ivy hung, smelled
of dust, our mouths lifting their black holes
like a tire I kept dreaming. Clenched
by mother and father who stank sweetly in sweat,

I sang and sang until the black ceiling
of our house seemed to sway and crack
and the tire skulled against my eyes
in time with the great clock in the far hall.
Hanging in darkness, like my sex, it made me listen.

3

One summer night here I came to fistfight Jim Jenrett,
whose house she had gone to, who is now no more

than a frail hand remembered on cheek, and I
was beer-brave, nearly wild with all
the dozen piling from cars. Jesus,
look at us in the ghost-flare of headlights,
pissing, taunting, boy-shadows, me hung
in the tire of my best friend spitting final threats.

So we passed, blinded, into the years, into the trees
holding their scars, half-healed, into the dark
where Jim, dunned by our words, went out
near dawn and stepped in the tire
and shied up the electric extension cord, noosed,
by the rope whose tire, burdened, ticked slowly.

4

Ghost-heart of this place, of dreams, I give you a shove
and sure enough I hear the tick and all that was
is, and a girl straightening her skirt walks
smack against you and screams. You know
who laughs, smoking in the shadows, don't you?

There are no headlights now, only the arc of blackness
gathering the hung world in its gullet. Blink
and maybe he's there, his great feet jammed
halfway in the hole of your heart,
gone halfway.

5

Where do they go who were with us on this dream road,
who flung themselves like seed under berry-black
nights, those faces black-clustered,
who could lean down and tell us
what love is and mercy and why now

I imagine a girl, mouth open in the sexual O, her hair
gone dull as soap scum, the husband grunting
as his fist smacks again, her scream
not out yet, nor the promise
she could never love anyone else.

I climb in the tire, swinging like a secret in the dark
woods surrounded by homelights of strangers.
She swore she loved me best.

In the church I imagined this place left forever behind
but it's with me as I try to see the road begin.
Blackberries on both sides blackly hang.
Trees, in blackness, leaned down at me.
When will they come, the headlights
washing over me like revelation,
the cars ticking and swirling like souls?

Once when my mother could not find me, they came here.
They said, "So this is it, the place." It was dark,
or nearly, and they said I might have died.
I asked them what being dead was like.
Like swinging at night, they joked, in the trees.

I shove my foot at the dirt, lifting off in blackness.
The whine of the rope is like a distant scream.
I think, so this is it. Really it.

for Robert Penn Warren

THE PORNOGRAPHY BOX

At eighteen, the U.S. Navy eye chart
memorized, reciting what was unseen,
my father enlisted for the duration.
At nineteen he caught a casual wave
wrong off Norfolk, our home, called
Hell by sailors. The landing craft
cast him loose and burst his knee.
He lived, and wore his rigid brace
without complaint, and never in this
life showed anyone his secret medal.
I stumbled into that brace and more
when I climbed to our sealed attic
the year a drunk blindsided him
to death in a ditch, and me to worse.

Today I watch my ten-year-old son race
over the faultless pages of *Playboy*,
ashamed I brought it home, imagining
his unasked questions have answers.
I remember the chairs I stacked
and climbed, the brace I put on
to see how it felt and, buried
deep in his sea chest, the livid
shapes shoved so far in a slit
of darkness a man could reach them
only hunched, on all fours. I clawed
through families of clothes discharged,
boxed ornaments for Christmas, to feel
the spooky silk of webs slickly
part on my face where blood rushed.

Trussed on their wide bed, my mother lay
surviving wreckage, stitched back
beyond secrets I hadn't guessed yet.
I shimmied through a dark hole

in the ceiling and listened to pine
rake the roof like a man's shuffle.
But he was dead, the box unlocked.
His flashlight pulsed through my body,
each glossy pose burning my eyes
that knew only airbrush innocence.
Sex rose in me like a first beard.
A woman with painted nails peeled
a foreskin, another held a man
kingly rigid at her tongue's tip.
I could not catch my breath.

I blinked at one spread on a table's
lace, grandmotherly clean and white.
Here might have been service for tea,
dainty cups, bread, a dish of cakes,
except she was in their place, child
in a middy suit. Behind her a vase
of daisies loomed, the parlor wall
sang *Home, Sweet Home* in needlepoint.
She might have been my young sister.
I remember the eyes, direct and flat,
as if she had died. Stockings knuckled
at her knees, her plaid skirt neatly
rolled on her chest. He, in three-piece
suit, cradled her calves in furred hands,
and placid as a navigator looked at
a window. He entered her like a knife.

After school, at night, weekend afternoons,
I raced to see them do it, legs cramped
in that freezing slot of darkness, gone
wobbly as a sailor into the country.
I came and went in the black tube
death opened for me like a new horizon.
In one sequence a black man held a pool
cue to a white woman, a black woman

grasped, grinning, black and white balls.
The uniforms of sailors were scattered,
wadded everywhere I looked. I smelled
the mothballs from my father's chest
when late at night I woke to vomit
at the clock's slit-eyed glowing.

How long does it go on, throbbing dreams,
waking obsessed with a hole in the air?
In Norfolk, from loaded cars, we spilled
at sailors passing alleys, asked for girls,
beer, good times, our cruel sucker-punch
a game played for strangers. *Bye-bye,
Seafood,* we yelled, then headed down
toward the Gaiety Theater and whores
bright as moths. We spit at mothers who
screamed *Fuck you, kid!* Crew-cut,
the secrets of our fathers, we cruised
those hopeless streets shiny as razors.
Neon flared like pus where they laughed
because we wanted love. Seeing now
my son bent to see I imagine at last

my father climbing before me in blackness,
with the tiny light a man carries, bent
on pained knees where I knelt also at
nameless images we each live to love
and fear. Exotics of the ordinary, one
dancer's crinolines flare around her
shaven rose. Another cooks in high heels,
a classmate suddenly gone from our town.
One on a patio reclines, not hiding her
one shorter leg. Each grins and burns
into memory, speaking in shy whispers,
all born to teach us what violation is.
At eighteen what fathers teach is wrong,
for the world is wrong, and only women
know why, their eyes dark as flat seas.

But it isn't eyes sons remember, blinded
by daylight on that raw breast, a thigh
where no face should be so open but is,
and is the mouth of the world's flesh
radiant in its rottenness, the secret
that leaves finally apart and other
all who learn to dream. In memory
I see how each nipple, cleft, face,
touch hissed our shame when accidentally
I became the boy-father of our house,
owner of obscenities. I hated us.
What else is the world but a box,
false-bottomed, where the ugly truths
wait and sail in the skins of ancestors?

Escaping them at last I left for worlds
unknown, but climbed first to his gifts,
carted that box and brace graveside,
and spilled those sweet faces down
under the tall Baptist spire. I spread
gasoline where we put him, then his
Navy Zippo lighter snapped it off.
Quick bodies coiled and flamed, ash
flecks rising like souls before me.
I gouged the remains in a trench
of churchly dirt, tried once to spit,
and turned in the dark for a bus.
In warm sun, his pea-coat was black
as the sea at midnight but I took it,
wore it, sweating for the cold to come.

Women smiled as if I was ripe, flushed
with cash from months at sea. *Welcome,
Anchor-clanker! We've waited for you!*
I was free, I thought, discharged from
Hell into the world that, for Christ's
sake, wanted me. Home gone, mother

drifting for a life. Maybe I'd write.
But was, after all, busy, holed up
with a nameless girl, the sharp blade
of her body a memory I still carry,
that darling who took my coat. But
by Easter I was ready, went. House sold,
mother maybe married, maybe in Florida,
they said. I wandered in cool sea winds,
as if on shore leave, until I came
cast up where my father was. Posters
of the nailed Jesus littered the grass.
A few crones kneeled faceless as stones
as if to serve the sun dying already.

I shivered, heard traffic hiss, walked
the old roads toward the shipyard and
wished I had our goddamn lost coat.
Boys yelled at me but no one stopped.
Freed, I felt myself. Who understands?
Hours I went in hard ways, night ahead,
my early beard bristling, dreaming what
gulls know. I came to a seedy hovel,
where films of flesh bared everything.
Among sailors I, a man, heard the siren
call us forward to sit with the heroes
under reels of lighted, loving women,
to dream in a theater called Art's House.
At love's edge, unbraced like my father,
I was nineteen, ready to take my step.

So we went in.

THE COLORS OF OUR AGE:
PINK AND BLACK

That year the war went on, nameless, somewhere,
but I felt no war in my heart,
not even the shotgun's ba-bam
at the brown blur of quail.
I abandoned brothers and fathers,
the slow march through marsh
and soybean nap where
at field's end the black shacks
noiselessly squatted under strings
of smoke. I wore flags of pink:
shirts, cuff links, belt, stitching.
Black pants noosed my ankles
into scuffed buck shoes.
I whistled Be-Bop-A-Lula
below a hat like Gene Vincent's.
My uniform for the light, and girls.

Or one girl, anyway, whose name I licked
like candy, for it was deliciously
pink as her sweater. Celia,
slow, drawling, and honey-haired,
whose lips hold in the deep mind
our malignant innocence of joy.
Among my children, on the first
of October, I sit for supper,
feet bare, tongue numb with smoke,
to help them sort out my history's
hysterical photographs. In pink
hands they take us up, fearless,
as we are funny and otherworldly.

Just beyond our sill two late hummingbirds,
black and white, fight for the feeder's
red, time-stalled one drop.

They dart in, drink, are gone,
and small hands part before me
an age of look-alikes, images
in time like a truce-wall
I stare over. The hot, warping
smell of concrete comes, fear
bitter as tear gas rakes
a public parking lot. Midtown
Shopping Center, Portsmouth, VA.,
the *Life* caption says, ink
faded only slightly, paper yellowing.

Everyone is here, centered, in horror
like Lee Oswald's stunned Ranger.
A 1958 Ford Victoria, finned,
top down and furred dice hung,
seems ready to leap in the background.
The black teenager, no name given,
glares at the lens in distraction.
Half-crouched, he shows no teeth,
is shirtless, finely muscled,
his arms extended like wings.
White sneakers with red stars
make him pigeon-toed, alert.
His fingers spread at his thighs
like Wilt Chamberlain trying
to know what moves and not look.

Three girls lean behind him, *Norcom H.S.*
stenciled on one who wears a circle
pin, another a ring and chain.
Their soft chocolate faces appear
glazed, cheeks like Almond Joys.
They face the other side, white,
reared the opposite direction,
barbered heads, ears, necks.
In between, a new shiny hammer

towers like an icon lifted
to its highest trajectory.
A Klan ring sinks into flesh,
third finger, left hand,
cuddling the hammer handle.

This man's shirt is white, soiled,
eagle-shaped, and voluminous. Collar up.
Each detail enters my eye like grit
from long nights without sleep.
I might have been this man, risen,
a small-town hero gone gimpy
with hatred of anyone's black eyes.
I watch the hummingbirds feint
and watch my children dismiss them,
focusing hammer and then a woman
tattooed under the man's scarred
and hairless forearm. The scroll
beneath the woman says *Freedom.*
Above her head, in dark letters
shaped like a school name on
my son's team jacket: *Seoul, 1954.*
When our youngest asks "Was that
black man the enemy?" I try
to answer: just a soldier, a war. . . .

I watch the feeder's tiny eye-round
drop, perfect as a breast
under the sweater of a girl
I saw go down, scuttling
like a crab, low, hands no use
against whatever had come to beat
into her silky black curls.
Her eyes were like quick birds
when the hammer nailed
her boyfriend's skull. Sick,
she flew against Penny's wall,

our hands trying to slap her sane.
In the Smarte Shoppe, acidly,
the mannequins smiled
in disbelief. Then I was
yanked from the light, a door

opened. I fell, as in memory I fall
to a time before that time.
Celia and I had gone to a field,
blanket spread, church done,
no one to see, no one expected.
But the black shack door opened,
the man who'd been wordless,
always, spoke, his words intimate
as a brother's, but banging out.
He grinned, he laughed, he wouldn't
stop. I damned his lippy face
but too late. He wiggled
his way inside my head.
He looked out, kept looking
from car window, school mirror,
from face black and tongue
pink as the clothes he wore.

Often enough Celia shrieked for joy,
no place too strange or obscene
for her, a child of the South.
When he fell, she squeezed
my hand and more, her lips came
fragrant at my ear. I see them
near my face, past the hammer.
But what do they say? Why, now,
do I feel the insuck of breath
as I begin to run—and from her?
Children, I lived there and wish
I could tell you this is only
a moment fading and long past.

But in Richmond, Charlotte, God knows
where else, by the ninth green,
at the end of a flagstone pathway
under pine shadow, a Buick waits
and I wait, heart hammering,
bearing the done and the undone,
unforgiven, wondering in what
year, in what terrible hour,
the summons will at last come.
That elegant card in the hand
below the seamless, sealed face—
when it calls whoever I am
will I stand for once and not run?
Or be whistled back, what I was, hers?

Out here, supper waiting, I watch my son
slip off, jacketed, time, place,
ancestors of no consequence to him,
no more than pictures a man carries
(unless a dunk shot inscribed).
For him, we are the irrelevance of age.
Who, then, will tell him of wars,
of faces that gather in his face
like shadows? For Christ's sake
look, I call to him, or you will
have to wait, somewhere, with us.
There I am, nearest the stranger
whose hammer moves quicker
than the Lord's own hand. I am
only seventeen. I don't smoke.
That's my friend Celia, kissing me.
We don't know what we're doing.
We're wearing pink and black.
She's dead now, I think.

TIDE POOLS

At dusk and long distance they are the mouths
to another world, caves of silence that speak
only in light, and tonight, family packed
for home travel, we take a last, slow route
over sand the sea has all day been stroking.
At driftwood the children stop, first veering
off wordlessly, and kneel to know some texture
of change, or stand merely to dream themselves
freely into the gathering shadows of the land.
As we go ahead of them, we imagine their hands
collecting what seems to have waited for each,
shells, starfish, agates sharp as a lover's eye.

Then we also drift apart, each following new
runnels the tide has left, and after a while
I see you hunched on a rock, almost part of it.
The light is nearly gone and the wind chills me
so I think of my father's whistle, ways it called
the sundered shadows of a family into the house.
But I don't whistle now, through the lips he made,
for somehow we have come where we may be apart
and whole. Instead I walk forward to understand
how each one is taken into the shapes of this place.

Then I find it, the deepest pool, its rock-vaulted
light bending as if alive in water faintly moving.
I see the lacy deceivers, the creatures disguised
as rock whose breath flutes in freshets like joy.
A killdeer cries from the black suck of the surf
and, though sweet, that darkness is not wanted.
This hole swells with the sun's final gold
and by it I learn to see what I always suspected—
the little unkillable pulsations of our life.

I gaze into the spooling depths, absorbed by all
that's bottomless, the open shells, the glitter
of hulls laid forever side by side like the dead
unwarily caught at last, perfect and untouchable.
How can I help sinking among those who loved us?

When finally I whistle there is almost no light,
but there's enough. You come then, invisible,
a sound made by the sand, a mingling of laughter,
and I duck under just in time, holding my breath.
Eyes burning, I watch as you bend to find me.
How I love your squeal of delight when I burst
up like a king from underground! Soon we're all
in naked and splashing, flying up like white birds.
The road home will be long and dark, the stars cold,
but collected like this we will be buoyed beyond
the dark snags and splinters of what we once were.

From *Goshawk, Antelope* (1979)

GOSHAWK, ANTELOPE

Against snowpeaks, that country of blue sedge and shimmer
of distance rising into his tiny skull full of desire, he
fell across my windshield, a dot at sixty, and I, half

looking for a place I had never seen, half dreaming rooms
where blind miles of light lie on framed family faces,

saw him before he was anything, a spot above the glassy road
and in my eye, acetylene burned by brightness and hours
of passage. I saw memory. He came

out of the clouded horizon like the hummed dark of whipped
phone wires and the quiet of first feathering shingles
in storm or in the hour of burial,

and dropped into absence where the antelope stood alive
at the fence of barbed wire, horns lifted slightly,
hovering on hooves' edge as if bored with the prospect
of leaps, long standing and still. The wind

darted dust gave no image beyond itself, puffballs turned
clockwise and counter-clockwise as he stood
changeless beneath that sudden whistle
of gray. I felt my heart

within those lovely shoulders flame and try to buck off
what the air had sent down as shapeless as obsession
and stopped my car, knowing already how
easily the talons dispossessed

all who, without illusions, lived. Dark and light bucked,
clung, shredded in me until I was again a boy on a fence,
hunched near the dream-contending world. But

someone far off was calling and I could not undream
what held me. Though I stood at last it was late,
too late. Someone called. The legs I had always
trusted broke and I fell from all chance
to change what was done or undone.

In Wyoming, in June, it was already starcold
and the mild blue of dusk beat back my mother's pain
when I saw him, small as a wind, shriek for the cliffs,
his dream gone, the aching wingless antelope risen
from a low mound of rocks, running from what was
unseen and there, like the red print of a hand

about to fall, for I was late, wishing to God for a tree
to hide under and see for once what had died
out of my life but would never leave
or come back as it had been—
like the slow growth of
an antelope's legs into freedom
from a black whirling dream. It was late,
there had been no sign, no reason to move

except the call that might have been only dreamed, but
once I stood under the keening moon that, in Wyoming,
owns all that is and I begged the stars not to come
gouging my bitter and motherless sleep

where I lay long and longed, as I do now over barbed wire,
for the peace of the night-gleaming peaks, the flare
of absence that came, falling into

the accusing goshawk face of my father in that dark room
where I walked too late, where the glowing fur-tufts
of candle shadows drift on her face and his

and what was held has become, suddenly, lost like breath.

UNDER THE SCRUB OAK, A RED SHOE

Wrapped in twisted brown stocking, rolled, strangled
in our grandmothers' nylon, it was wedged at the heart
of what little cool shade ever accumulated there.
You would have to walk out of your way, back
along an arroyo twisting, empty as first memory,
back from the road out of town so far the sky
signals another world. To find it you do that,

though, in any case, you are simply walking: it appears,
something red shining through the gray-green glaze
of stunted limbs. If you were looking for a lost
child, steps deliberate and slow, you might see it.
Otherwise you will go on. Tonight it shines out,
having waited long to reveal itself, like an eye
in the darkness, and I innocently look into

its moment, imagining why it lacks a slender heel which
must, once, have nailed many boys against a wall
where she walked. I kneel and pick it up
as you would, hearing though it is noon
the moony insects cry around her, hearing also
the nylon like another skin scrape against my skin,

feeling the sound of its offslipping from her shaven calf,
a screech like the full-bellied hawk's when he floats.
In the arroyo no one could have seen her stop,
not as drunk as she pretended, sitting long
and, in time, methodically undressing, beyond
thinking now, placing her bundled shoe with care.
She must have been small. She would bear the usual

bruises, we would have had no fear of any we might add,
when we stood smoking by the wall, catcalling lightly.
It would have been one of those nights the breath
aches to be free of itself, of the body, then

she appeared in that red like first cactus buds,
something clearly wrong with her but that, by God,
no concern of any red-blooded boy she might want.

In the junked car someone squealed, someone
rose and fell. There were no names. I did not mean
whatever I said, but said it because she was so small.
She lay inside her fear, she shivered on her back.
Such moments we tell ourselves to walk away from,
and we do, as now I have walked in my hoping

for absence, but there is no absence, just
what waits, like a shoe, to reach, to say please
as best it can to whoever comes along, as if it
meant forgiveness, and love, as if any weather
that red skin endured was only the bruise
you might have kissed and might not yet refuse.

HAWKTREE

Tonight in the hills there was a light
that leaped out of the head
and yellow longing of a young boy.
It was Spring and he had walked
through the toy-littered yards
to the edge of town, and beyond.
In the tall spare shadow of a pine
he saw her standing, her skin
whiter than the one cloud
each day loaned to the long sky,
whiter even than the moon.
But she would not speak to one
who kept her name to himself
when boys laughed in the courtyard.
He watched her burn like a candle
in the cathedral of the needles.
After a while he saw the other light,
the sun's leveling blister, bring
its change to her wheaten hair.
In growing dark he waited, certain
she would hear the pine's whisper,
counting on Nature's mediation.
But she would not speak and even
as he watched she vanished.
Slowly he knew his arms furred
with a fragrant green darkness
and as the moon cut its swaths
on the ground, as trucks rooted
along the road of colored pleasures,
he felt his feet pushing through
his shoes, his hair going stiff.
He could hear her laugh, could see
her long finger loop a man's ear.
But this did not matter. Already

he felt himself sway a little
in the desert wind, in the wordless
gnarling he became and knew then.

WAKING AMONG HORSES

So then in the morning we would wake,
the steam of marsh summer on us,
sheets kicked back, blackbirds calling,
and out of whatever dream
we had been floating inside
our mouths would open and lazily
gulp the air as if this were forever
the water of love's sailing,
and we would begin to listen.

Your hair in my hands drifting,
the dark odor of pine pitch, that
sizzle of sun on our skin
comes back now like the bell
of your breast turning me
until I hear the slow saw drone
brassy and belligerent, cutting
down the distances of salt water.
In our words we held the child,
almost, saw the face we gave it
conceived by whatever sent
us to learn how faith can fail.

I would lie asking what face
looked in when the sparrows flew
at windows where we swelled
in this birth of the imagination,
and you would cry no, no,
as if the dream we rode bolted
like the farmer's horse, so
we became two falling.
Whoever saw our one face
at the high attic window
might have thought we lived
alone in that blue emptiness.

Mornings the gray stallion stood
to see what we wanted, or say
what the world must give him.
We would lie in the split vision
of the moment memory
entered us, as love does,
and we heard the horses
mating in those June fields.

All I want is to know how
it can come back, the place,
naked whistles, blowing birds
like sun-sparks struck, you
in that not knowing where,
in that fatigued swoop of joy.
We'd surely rise again, and
fall, startled by fate we saw
dropping each mare down
on dirt's hardness. We knew
nothing breaks or opens but
to show all beginning again.

August, on the Rented Farm

In this season, through the clear tears
of discovery, my son calls me
to an abandoned barn. Among
spiders' goldspinning and the small
eulogies of crickets, he has entered
the showering secret of our lives,
and the light fur of something
half-eaten mats his hands.
Later, on a rotting length
of pine, we sit
under the star-brilliance
of birds fretting the light.
Under them, dreamless,
we have come to cast
our lot with songs
of celebration.
All afternoon we sit and become
lovers, his hand in mine
like a bird's delicate wing.
Everywhere sparrows go down
to the river for the sweet
tears of communion. Soon,
in the yellow last light,
we will begin again to speak
of that light in the house
that is not ours, that is only
what we come to out of the fields
in the slow-plunging knowledge
of words trying to find a way home.

WAVING

In the backyard, by the stilled
oscillations of the cheap
metal fence defined
by the weight of children,
the small maple
waves in the first
gusts of a fall day.
Behind breath-frosted
glass, hearing far off
my child's cry, I
see this waving become
my father's thick arms.
He waves at the ball game
where players swarm
at his call. One spits.
He waves from the nose
of a rowboat, drunk
with fish, unashamed.
He waves at the black
end of a treeless street
where my mother has turned
from the house, crying.
He waves on a little hill
above the playground,
his whistle shearing
over each knuckle
of asphalt. When I stop
running, out of breath,
he is still there, waving,
and I am waving, beating
the air with my arms,
sore and afraid,
and there is no wind, only
the brilliant distance
like a fence between us,
waving and waving.

A Moment of Small Pillagers

That flock of starlings hewing the air
above the orchard is nothing
but the strangling of desire.
I know their country is nowhere
and would not throw a single stone
against such beautiful longing.
They have walked out to be
at the heart of our bodies,
and cannot find what they want,
or even a gleam from the gone sun.
Under them I bend down quietly
and pick up a black feather
as if it were the dropped scarf
of my sleeping daughter. Holding
this for hours, I find myself
unable to say a simple word
true or false, until I become
the little thing the body is
in the hiding fur of a woods.
Then I look across the hedgerows
at the foreign light of my house.
Somewhere in the distance of dark
a voice is calling my name,
but not too loud, and I want
to fly up and gather the last
radiance of the sun and take it
like a song down to her mouth.
Oh daughter, in the thick trees
where fruit bruises beyond joy,
I hunch among the starlings.

for Mary Catherine Smith

THE DARK EYES OF DAUGHTERS

Flying from the end of my
boot, my daughter's cat,
and the tame quail gone
up in a spatter of feathers,
to leave me turning there
as the dew dulls out, bare
shoulders flushed from that
quick sprint, the back door
still banging like a flattened
wheel of memory. I think
I can hear the world grind.
I feel like a man in a car
who's just dropped something
barely alive on a quiet street.
I am saying *Please, please,*
and only mean I want to go
on wherever I am going.
I want the trees to remain
a close forgiving green
without that hot light
ahead banging down hard. I
don't want, for God's sake,
to hear this slow gouging
of sparks that the world is,
the intense unloosening stare
in the cat's eyes as I loom
out of the sudden stillness,
the fixed and believing
pupils of the child startled
to see what cruelty is, always
to know this first dream of
love's division. I am crying
Please, oh please—not
wanting this to happen yet,
sun the color of a cat falling

on her struck face that is
learning to mouth these words
without end, with only one
beginning already long lost
like pawprint or feather
where grass goes stunningly
dead and pain, like flint, strikes.

for Lael Cornwell Smith

PINE CONES

Any way you hold them, they hurt.
What's the use, then?

Once in our backyard, by a sparrow's hidden
tremor there in the green wish of spruce,
a full but unfolded body hung.

It bore every color of the world and was sweet
beyond measure. The canyon wind banged
at this then went elsewhere.

Something happened that night.
The sparrow seems to have seen what it was.

Look at him huddled, mistakably some other shadow,
the sly outlines of his body almost blue as spruce,
the sun like a big wall nearby,

and you stepping through it, big, so big
he would almost give up his only wish.

Almost. Almost. Almost.

Isn't this the way hearts beat in the world,
the way pine cones fall in the night
until they don't?

When you pick them up, as children do,
the tiny spot appears in your palm,
red as the sun's first blink
of love.

And that sticking, unabidable tar.

Rain Forest

The green mothering of moss knits shadow and light,
the silence and call of each least bird where
we walk and find there are only a few words
we want to say: water, root, light, and love,
like the names of time. Stunned from ourselves
we are at tour's tail end, our guide long gone,
dawdling deep in what cannot be by any human
invented, a few square miles of the concentric
universe intricate as the whorls of fingertips.
The frailest twigs puff and flag in the giantism
of this elaborate grotto, and we are the dream,
before we know better, of an old grotesque
stonecutter who squats under a brow of marble.
We have entered the huge inward drift behind
his eyes and wait to become ourselves. We stare
through limpid eyes into the vapor-lit past
where breath, wordlessly, like a near river
seams up, seams in and out around darkness.
Somewhere far back in the hunch of shadows,
we stood by this wall of vines, and he, angry,
froze us in our tracks and the blade of belief.
That tree there bore the same long slithering
of light from a sky he owned. Disfigured now,
its trunk rises thick and black as a monument
that rings when struck. Here the hiking path,
a crease, stops, then spirals around into stumps.
Our party has gone that way, stumbling quietly.
From time to time, someone calls out but we know
only the words whispered from the wall of leaves:
water, root, light, and love. We stand silent
in the earliest air remembered, hearing at last
the distant and precise taps of the mallet
until our clothes, as if rotted, fall away
and the feckless light fixes us on the column
of our spines. Without warning, we begin to dance,

a bird cries, and another. Our feet seem to spark
on the hard dirt as we go round the black tree
and for no reason we know we see ourselves
throwing our heads back to laugh, our gums
and teeth shiny as cut wood, our eyes marbled,
straining to see where it comes from, that
hoarse rasp of joy, that clapping of hands
before which we may not speak or sing or ever stop.

From *Cumberland Station* (1977)

ON A FIELD TRIP AT FREDERICKSBURG

The big steel tourist shield says maybe
fifteen thousand got it here. No word
of either Whitman or one uncle
I barely remember in the smoke
that filled his tiny mountain house.

If each finger were a thousand of them
I could clap my hands and be dead
up to my wrists. It was quick
though not so fast as we can do it
now, one bomb, atomic or worse,
the tiny pod slung on wingtip,
high up, an egg cradled
by some rapacious mockingbird.

Hiroshima canned nine times their number
in a flash. Few had the time
to moan or feel the feeling
ooze back in the groin.

In a ditch I stand
above Mayre's Heights, the bookish
faces of Brady's fifteen-year-old
drummers, before battle, rigid
as August's dandelions
all the way to the Potomac
rolling in my skull.

If Audubon came here, the names
of birds would gush, the marvel
single feathers make
evoke a cloud, a nation,
a gray blur preserved
on a blue horizon, but

there is only a wandering child,
one dark stalk snapped off
in her hand. Hopeless teacher,
I take it, try to help her
hold its obscure syllables
one instant in her mouth,
like a drift of wind
at the forehead, the front door,
the black, numb fingernails.

Blues for Benny "Kid" Paret

For years I've watched the corners for signs.
A hook, a jab, a feint, the peekaboo prayer of forearms,
anything for the opening, the rematch I go on dreaming.
What moves can say your life is saved?

As I backpedaled in a field the wasps' nest waited,
playing another game: a child peeps out of
my eyes now, confused by a rage of stinging,
wave after wave rising as I tell my fists to hurt me,
hurt the pain. I take my own beating, God help me

it hurts. Everything hurts, every punch darts,
jolts, enters my ears, bangs my temples. Who hurts
a man faster than himself? There was a wall I
bounced on, better than ropes. I was eleven years old.

In that year I saw the fog
turn aside and rise from the welts you were
to run away with its cousin the moon. They smacked
your chest and crossed your arms because you fell down
while the aisles filled with gorgeous women, high heels
pounding off like Emile, the Champion, who planted
his good two feet and stuck, stuck, stuck, stuck
until your brain tied up your tongue and your breath.

Somebody please, please I cried,
make them go away, but the ball in my hand was
feverish with the crackling light. I could not let go
as I broke against the wall. I was eleven years old.

Benny Paret, this night in a car ferrying
my load of darkness like a ring no one escapes,
I am bobbing and weaving in fog split only by a radio
whose harsh gargle is eleven years old, a voice in the air

telling the night you're down, counting time,
and I hear other voices, corners with bad moves
say *Get up you son of a bitch, get up and fight!* But you don't
get up again in my life and the only life you had is gone

with the moon I remember sailing down on your heart
where you lay in blood, waiting, photo flashes all snapped,
eyes open to take whatever is yet to come, jabs, hooks, cross
breaking through the best prayer you ever lifted to dump
you dizzied and dreamless in the green soft grass.

How to Get to Green Springs

Nobody knows exactly when it fell off the map
or what the pressures were on its flooding river.
The hedge, the tottering mailbox—gone. That dimple
of light from the bicycle that raised itself to creak
at noon across a clattering bridge names my father.
His blood silent as a surging wish drags this town
lost through my body, a place I can get back to only
by hunch and a train whistle that was right on time.

But time and trains were never right in Green Springs,
West Virginia. What color could map the coal's grime,
shacks shored against the river every March, mail
left to rot because no one answered to occupant?
Farmers low on sugar cursed the heat and left cigars
boys would puff back to clouds where they dreamed
of girls naked as their hands under outfield flies.
Scores were low. There were no springs for the sick.
Women lined their walls with the Sears catalog, but
the only fur they ever had was a warbled rabbit.
To get here think of dirt, think of night leaking,
the tick of waterbugs, a train held in Pittsburgh.

CUMBERLAND STATION

Gray brick, ash, hand-bent railings, steps so big
it takes hours to mount them, polished oak
pews holding slim hafts of sun, and one
splash of the *Pittsburgh Post-Gazette*. The man
who left Cumberland gone, come back, no job
anywhere. I come here alone, shaken
the way I came years ago to ride down
mountains in Big Daddy's cab. He was
the first set cold in the black meadow.

Six rows of track, photographed, gleam, rippling
like water on walls where famous engineers steam, half
submerged in frothing crowds with something
to celebrate and plenty to eat. One's mine,
taking children for a free ride, a frolic
like an earthquake. Ash cakes his hair.
I am one of those who walked uphill
through flowers of soot to zing
scared to death into the world.

Now whole families afoot cruise South Cumberland
for something to do, no jobs, no money for bars,
the old stories cracked like wallets.

This time there's no fun in coming back. The second
death. My roundhouse uncle coughed his youth
into a gutter. His son slid on the ice,
losing his need to drink himself
stupidly dead. In this vaulted hall
I think of all the dirt poured down
from shovels and trains and empty pockets.
I stare into the huge malignant headlamps
circling the gray walls and catch a stuttered
glimpse of faces stunned like deer on a track.

Churning through the inner space of this godforsaken
wayside, I feel the ground try to upchuck and I dig
my fingers in my temples to bury a child
diced on a cowcatcher, a woman smelling
alkaline from washing out the soot.
Where I stood in that hopeless, hateful room
will not leave me. The scarf of smoke I saw
over a man's shoulder runs through me
like the sored Potomac River.

Grandfather, you ask why I don't visit you
now you have escaped the ticket-seller's cage
to fumble hooks and clean the Shakespeare reels.
What could we catch? I've been sitting in the pews
thinking about us a long time, long enough to see
a man can't live in jobless, friendless Cumberland
anymore. The soot owns even the fish.

I keep promising I'll come back, we'll get out,
you and me, like brothers, and I mean it.
A while ago a man with the look of a demented cousin
shuffled across this skittery floor and snatched up
the *Post-Gazette* and stuffed it in his coat
and nobody gave a damn because nobody cares
who comes or goes here or even who steals
what nobody wants: old news, photographs
of dead diesels behind chipped glass.

I'm the man who stole it and I wish you were here
to beat the hell out of me because what you said
a long time ago welts my face and won't go away.
I admit it isn't mine, even if it's nobody's.
Anyway, that's all I catch today—bad news.
I can't catch my nephew's life, my uncle's,
Big Daddy's, yours, or the ash-haired kids'
who fell down to sleep here after the war.

Outside new families pick their way along tracks
you and I have walked home on many nights.
Every face on the walls goes on smiling,
and, Grandfather, I wish I had the guts
to tell you this is a place I hope
I never have to go through again.

THE SPRING POEM

Everyone should write a Spring poem!
   —Louise Glück

Yes, but we must be sure of verities
such as proper heat and adequate form.
That's what poets are for, is my theory.
This then is a Spring poem. A car warms
its rusting hulk in a meadow; weeds slog
up its flanks in martial weather. April
or late March is our month. There is a fog
of spunky mildew and sweaty tufts spill
from the damp rump of a back seat. A spring
thrusts one gleaming tip out, a brilliant tooth
uncoiling from Winter's tension, a ring
of insects alongside, working out the Truth.
Each year this car, melting around that spring,
hears nails trench from boards and every squeak sing.

BOATS

On the Poquoson River

Rounding a slip of the marsh, the boat skids
under me and the propeller whines naked, digs,
then shoots me forward. A clapper rail
disappears in reeds and one white crane,
shaken from his nap, blinks and holds.

He makes me think of the Lost Tribe of Virginia,
as if the screech of insects was the Jew's
harp in John Jacob Niles's mouth. Redwings cry,
hidden like women mending nets too fine to see.

A creek opens its throat and I enter, dragging
down to hear the wake's slip-slop behind me,
thinking of the man who warned me people
were the same everywhere, lost and wondering

how they came to the life no one else wanted.
Sweet Jesus, he was right. Now he lies
in this sodden ground for the first time
in his life and I do not know even where.

Today is no different, the waters flood hulks
of empty houses, leaving beer cans to gleam
under the grinding moon. The first stalks
of narcissus break the ground with gold
though March still means tonight to freeze.

I know this place, its small mustering of facts
wind-worn and useless, real and repeated, the same
anywhere. At the end the creek leads to a room,
one placid boat swinging at a stick, pines sieving

air, the cleat ringing like small jewelry.

i.m. James Wright

The Cunner in the Calotype

You need to know these boats, cunners, square
of bow and stern, never painted, always with a bottle
floating where the bilge is always rank and deep.
Sometimes they hold the sun like a butter tub but
nobody ever stepped a sail in one. They're used
to ferry out to where oyster scows squat, sere
and long as a lovely woman's thigh in a man's dream.
You need to ask why they lie cracked, sucking salt
water through the reed tubes, what has happened
to shove them back into the center of the marsh
where the screech of gnats goes out when a fisherman,
desperate in the end, shoves his finger in his ear.
You need to hear the slow toll of rope-ends, mossed
like drifting arms, the bell-cry of cleat and chained
transom stained a hundred hues by years of seas.

When bulldozers come to take the marsh, slapping down
layers of asphalt, when the all-temperature malls rise,
when women of the garden club cease their designing,
cunners will be gone, claimed by antique freaks, smashed
for scrap, the creeks leveled, the sun deceived with
only absence flashing in the heat. Once unemployed,
no swimming boys will sink them for a joke, no wind
whip and toss them in a storm or leave them in a tree.
Must fishermen exchange their daily lacks for jobs
behind counters? What rower of boats loves dirt?
What you get for one wouldn't pay for a week's beer.
But for them, fathers, you need to know I give you
this cunner of my place, its hand-hacked bottom whole
yet, the smell of crabs rank all over, a man's hat
floating in the black water as if mislaid, going down.

Aubrey Bodine's crosswater shot of Menchville,
Virginia: a little drama composing a little water,
specifically, the Deep Creek flank of the James.
Two-man oyster scows lie shoulder to shoulder,
as if you walk them, one land to another,
no narrow channel hidden in the glossy middle
like a blurred stroke, current grinning at hulls.
It is an entirely eloquent peace, with lolling
ropes and liquid glitter, this vision of traffic
and no oystermen in sight. Clearly Bodine is
not Matthew Brady catching the gropes frozen
at Fredericksburg with a small black box. So
well has he balanced the Mennonite church, yachts,
and country club, dignity's spare smell seeps.
His wide-angle lens foregrounds the bent teeth
of oyster tongs. Perhaps no Sunday bells toll.

Above the last boat, the flat-faced store squats
at the end of the dirt road as if musing over
accounts receivable. No doubt it has weathered
years of blood spilling. A spotted hound lifts
his nose above what must be yesterday's trash,
his white coat luminous at deep foliage. What
Bodine fails to show is the dog turning to lope
uphill under that screen of poplars, behind fat
azaleas that hide the county jail and drunks
starting to smell water's way out. Thumping
his noisy wife out a window, an oysterman cries
she cut him more than twice, madly mourning
their boy drowned twenty years. If he knew
Bodine had stood to snap the spot the boy died,
if we said a camera's yawn could suck back years
of his worst sailing shame, he would turn away.

He would whistle up mates in dignity's dust
and he would spit in his fists and would tell
his nameless black cellmate there are many men
for whom the world is neither oyster nor pearl.

NIGHT FISHING FOR BLUES

At Fortress Monroe, Virginia,
the big-jawed Bluefish, ravenous, sleek muscle slamming
at rock, at pier legs, drives into Chesapeake shallows,
convoys rank after rank, wheeling through
flume and flute of blood, something
like hunger's throb hooking
until you hear it and know them there,
the family.
                    Tonight, not far from where Jefferson Davis
hunched in a harrowing cell, gray eyes quick
as crabs's nubs, I come back over planks
deep drummed under boots years ago, tufts of hair

floating at my eyes, thinking it is right
                    to pitch through tideturn and mudslur
                    for fish with teeth like snapped sabers.
                    In blue crescents of base lights, I cast hooks

baited with Smithfield ham: they reel, zing,
plummet, coil in corrosive swirls, bump on
scum-skinned rocks. No skin divers prowl here,
                    visibility an arm's length, my visions

hand-to-hand in the line's warp. A meat-baited
lure limps through limbs nippling the muck,
silhouettes, shoots forward, catches a cruising Blue
sentry's eye, snags, and sets

case-hardened barbs. Suddenly, I am not alone:
                    three negroes plump down in lawn chairs, shudder,
                    cast quick into the black pod slopping under us. One

                    ripples with age, a grandmotherly obelisk,

her breath puffing like a coal stove. She swivels
heavily, chewing her dark nut, humming gospel,
then spits thick juice like a careful chum.

When I yank the first Blue
she mumbles, her eyes roll far out on the black
blue billowing of the sea. I hear her cant
            to Africa, a cluck in her throat, a chain

song from the fisherman's house. I cannot
understand her yet. Bluefish pour at me in squads.
I haul two, three at a time, torpedoes, moon-shiners,
jamming my feet into the splintered floor, battling
whatever comes. Fathers, we have waited
a whole life for this minute. Dreams

            graven on cold cell walls, Blues walk over

our heads, ground on back-wings, grind their teeth.
They splash rings of blue and silver around us, chevrons
of lost battalions. I can smell the salt of many ocean
runners, and now she hollers *I ain't doing so bad
for an old queen!* No time to answer. Two

            car-hoods down her descendents swing

moonsleek arms, exotic butterflies: I hear them
pop beer cans, the whoosh released like stale breath
through a noose no one remembers. We hang
fast flat casts, artless, no teasing fishers,
beyond the book-bred lures, the pristine streams,
speeded-up, hungry, almost machines wound
too far, belts slipped, gears gone, momentum

            hauling us to race at each other, winging

wildly as howitzers. Incredibly it happens: I feel
the hook hammer and shake and throw my entire weight
to dragging, as if have caught the goddamndest

           Blue in the Atlantic. She screams: *Oh my God!*
Four of us fumbling in beamed headlight and blue
arcs overhead cut the hook from her face. Gnats
nag us: I put it in deep and it must be gouged out
like old hate. When it is free, I hear Blues

not dead flop softly. I whisper it's luck
she could see us. She mops blood blued over
gold-lined teeth and opens her arms so her dress
           billows like a caftan. She wants

nothing but to fish. I hand her a pole, then cast
as far as I can. She pumps, wings a sinker and hooks
into flashing slop and reels hard. In one instant both

           our lines leap rigid as daguerreotypes. We

have caught each other but keep on, pushed by blue
ghosts that thrash in the brain's deep cull.
We reel shadows until we see there is nothing,
then sit on the shaky pier like prisoners. Coil
by coil we trace the path of Bluefish-knots backward,
           unlooping, feeling for holes, testing,

slapping gnats like small fears. Harried, unbound,
at last we leap to fish again. But now a gray glow
shreds with the cloud curtain, an old belly-fire
           guts the night. Already the tide humps

on itself. Lights flicker like campfires in duty windows
at Ft. Monroe. She hooks up, saying *Sons they done
let us go.* I cast once more but nothing bites.

Everywhere the circle of Blues stiffens

in flecks of blood. We kneel, stuff styrofoam
boxes with blankets of ice, break their backs
to keep them cold and sweet, the woman
showing us what to do. By dawn the stink has passed
out of our noses. We drink beer like family.

All the way home thousands of Blues fall from my head,
falling with the gray Atlantic, and a pale veiny light
fills the road with sea-shadows that drift in figure

eights, knot and snarl and draw me forward.

From *The Fisherman's Whore* (1974)

THE FISHERMAN'S WHORE

Like gentle swells
of corn rows that will never fade
from golf course fairways,
        or burial mounds,
dead boats in low silhouettes

        rise in dawn sweat
from black marsh mud beaded where
the town's trash leaches in.
        Water blisters blue.
The fathers' worn whores wait.

        Along swing-laden
stoops of whitewashed houses you
can hear the lacy swamp grass
        angrily hiss, bladed
now in winter's changing wind.

        Rattling in throats,
hunched fishermen sag against
the caved-in hulls once more,
        all gray as the lies
they scatter to the flood tide.

        Mother-of-pearl dots
their flanks. Scale-buttons, badges of
shells flash sun like jewels from
        curves no woman has.
Plank-seep blood-freckles them.

        Rust bullet-holes out
of pine, yet few joints give wholly.
Time-wombs, ulcered, too
        weak to bear men
safe on thudding seas, to some

they seem yet to sail.
Young men, here listening, stand
in dreams, waking, or lie up
on thighs of chines.
Sun on fathers makes its fable.

Every day a boy goes.
Another, bicycle stacked by creek,
faces the wind that paints him in
love's raw grip, her
touch now giving all he imagines.

Near the Docks

There was a fire in the night.
Across the street I slept among the others
as the ash snowed upon small pines.
I slept owning nothing, a child ignorant
of fortune's blistering story, the playful
flash in the dark, the unseen smolder
that would leave us revealed, though
unchanged as the black earth.
I said my prayers for luck
like the man trying to live
in two houses, hoping for time
to leave the old one of his fathers,
its windows with weariness fogged.
The other was half-built, roofless,
green timbers going gray in sun
like a vision that would not be done.

I had climbed there all summer to smoke
after the hours when I would find him
hunched on his wooden stool. Each
morning, halfway between the houses,
on his tongue would be the story
of how they came and of the sea,
his hands weaving wire to a trap,
making careful seams to catch
cunning scuttlers. I saw his wife
already had begun to hang her wash,
its shapes rueful, steaming, ghostly
in sunflare. That day a mongrel
lapped from the ruts of the fire trucks.

I thought little was changed by fire,
only his toolshed limp as a black sail
left in a heap, and that new hole
in the landscape. This was a poor place

where no one came, luckless, desperate,
eternal as guilt. I was the same
as the day before. In silence
I greeted that old one. Now I remember
seeing also, as if for the first time,
the shocking gray face of the sea
was his, fixed, in one quick glance.
It loomed up human and beautiful
as far off the figures of boats
crossed, worked, and seemed to sink
while they burned in the sullen sun.

Oyster Boats at Plum Tree Cove

A boy says among the broken hulls,
I have been away growing old
at the heart of another country
where there are no boats crumbling,
or small crabs with scuttling tools.
These pines warped with early snow,
this light that slopes and breaks
as the sea slides, sloughing
against your air and earth-worn
flanks: I had loosed the dead
from memory but, coming back
confused, I find them waiting
here at the sea's rattling edge.

It is too much to speak to them, yet
to them through you I bow, politely
soiled and whiskered, wanting to drink,
to stand under the hard throats
with whiskey at Plum Cove, among
the booted ones with plaid shirts
and large loving hands. But wanting
is not enough: I ask you for words
hooked in your holds. I want
to say what you know, who groan
or roll where the village sleeps off
its wild hours among new azaleas.
I taste rank air. Wind pushes a wave.

The Shark in the Rafters

Under the stuttered snatch of the winch
they draw him by pulley and wheel,
the net-fouler unaccountably caught.
Slower than the night tracking
the sun through warm furrows
he rises into the open fishhouse
where the sea's womb-blue lies
at a hole hacked in the house floor.

Not this mechanical screech but siren's
reedy crying blown out brings
the women from a darkness
of pine, through swamp grass
where age-ruptured boats hulk,
buried, decaying. Widows, wives,
they bluntly gaze like lovers
here at the land's last house,
no windows, no doors, just
the sun's tall fire, the wing
of shark swaying under the roof.

Beautiful, they watch the terrible
jaws jammed open again, the hook
spooning out the man's leg-stump,
blood-sluice flowing below them
into the minnow seeded water,
each surprised to feel risen
inside a finger's forbidden
touch: this hide is all
between them and sun's boil.
To open it at last, one
climbs with his knife, cheered
by the girls whose thighs burn

merely standing as one by one each
gore-tooth is made astonishingly

large, the great eye gouged,
tossed to small feeders, flesh
stripped out in tongues, a way
cut inside by bright coils
of bone, then there it is:
the heart, plain, dark
as a clock on a nightstand.
They cut it out, laughing,
and offer it up in parts
that fly like birds to hands.

Now the men grunt, hammerheaded,
as they pass dull meat to the women.
In an eyeblink gobbets, bloodied,
bob in ooze the tide draws
back to its salt slime, little
knots of flesh adrift in sun.
No one gives the shark a name
as they lug it home, hungry
at day's end, oddly buzzing
as if electrified by stars.

In rooms heavy with the smell of
saltwater, daughters of daughters
stand close, whisper the tale:
an unwed woman is remembered,
hung over the splintered floor
in her bed, moon-shadow on her
blank as a clock. The eyes grow
luminous, lips pull back, teeth
shine in each soft one turning
hard beside her sister. One
peels the flesh, knife quick.
One fries, hands blistering.
Speaking of death, they begin
where the heart was beating to
pieces, the mouth hugely open.

for James Applewhite

ROOSTER SMITH'S LAST LOG CANOE

Mariner's Museum, Newport News, Virginia

Suspended in a vast pendulum of blue light
they keep alive the legends of boats,
the whole evolution of their making

huddled beneath the giant bust
of an American Eagle
whose wings filter the sun, whose

talons press and hold a huge brass dial
which spreads time on the floor
like moss in a cove.

Each step drops a man deeper in the Eagle's
eye, and there is one room Rooster
lives in, a man recognizable

by the scars on his hand or the shy
shadowy way he poses by his last boat,
as if he is saying again and again

this one is for you, this I have well built.
His arm bends into the curved bow
and the chines of heartwood.

On the wall there is a series of photographs
as precise and stiff as half-inch
sheets of James River ice.

In the first, a tree, fully leafed, rippled
sunshine on the slack water in the rear.
Nothing else has happened.

Rooster stands then by the corpse of an ancient
trunk, his saw baring its teeth like a fish.
He seems sad or winded.

Two men, one shadowed and grim, one lighter, lean
into the hollowed body of wood, their faces
turned up, surprised. The river is flat.

A keel rises in the bladed reeds. Ribs glisten.
The men lean on each other; wood chips
fleck the gray earth like stars.

A mast leads the eye to the center of the river
where specks seem loose, errant, whipped
by winds. No men appear.

On Model-A wheels, she strains at the edge of
Deep Creek Point. Pines like massive wings
hover over the hull. Rooster looks

to the next photograph, where she is under way.
He is missing, and the other man.
It is marked THE LAST BAY CANOE.

Under the final frame, the green hull sleeps
in its chocks, a tree full of warm light,
its body groaning for water. Your hand,

which once swung from Rooster's calloused fingers,
presses the chines to feel where blade,
fire, sweat made their marks.

Some things do not show in two-dimensional gloss:
pain in the chest, arm-breaking knots.
Northeast storms escape this room.

But with the hand speaking to the wood, under
the Eagle's time-splintering gaze, a wind
in a wind begins to blow.

You listen the way a child does, feeling in
the open chinks and caulkless seams
for Rooster's empty bottles.

Everything is exactly as it was, the dark stain
on the stern seat, the heavy chain links
played out, the bird circling overhead.

In that dusk-deflected light you are told it keeps
your grandmother's torn skirt, a piece
the sea blew on in wood's belly.

HAMMY'S BOAT CIRCLING
THROUGH THE MOON

This is the dream I have had
three nights in a row, a story
of the eldest son, who can't
come in from Chesapeake Bay.

Hammy's skin is slippery.
It stinks and glitters.
He is drunk again.
He floats, he cannot swim.

Beulah's hull, her black nets
hung like a woman's veil,
wears forty-five skins of paint,
not a year scraped or sanded.

Calm as a snake, the Bay
moves, phosphor on dark coils,
and moonlight, a spray
of moss pulling seaward like hair.

Beulah starts to spin, its one-cycle
thumper tracking over ripples
thrown by a locked rudder,
then bubbles, then hair floating.

I know he's here, dog-paddling,
drunk, calling his boat back,
dog to the hand he lifts
in the stairless night. She

dreams herself slowly around, is
bobbing like a girl, and still
out among moon-beauties,
at Bay star-windows, she rounds.

March Storm,
Posquoson, Virginia, 1963

For three days the wind blew northeast,
reeds huddled underwater, bent back and down,
like birds with their heads bowed
in a winged darkness. The tide
held, came on slowly, not impelled
by high slopes to flood and churn
through narrows, but a lapping gray
light mounting the back steps: it came
unnoised, settled among our shoes
at the corners of closets, from
under sofas and rockers licked out
to sweep the rooms free of dust,
socks, dead mice, whatever would swim.

When the sun broke the fourth day's wake
the water retreated in silence,
the oyster boats sank, gentled
in the tops of the pines,
rudders lolling like dogs's tongues.
Stunned like drunks gone out
into abrupt noon light, we walked
through the fields, crowded
under the hulls' intimate shadows
to lift up our arms and show proof
of the scarred wounds seen at last
where we had always felt them.
All around us delicate seagrass
uprooted, rose and billowed until
each of us, lean as skeletal fish,
darted off as if to escape
the closing net of oncoming night.

LAEL'S SONG

New child, often I think of your
birth as the nights of winter
grow ghostly in my brain.
With you I hear the chuf, chuff

of boxcars bumping toward towns
whose waiting night lights
not even the dead could cause
to flicker. When I feel you kick

in your mother's swollen house,
my backbone bows, I wake
thinking now it is time to go
where the long night is glowing

with names, with things we want
to say. Already we have carried
the one pale face of your brother
from the darkness where you are.

Our hearts soar at your coming.
You must kick on, be ready for
the edge of the world breaks,
cars thudding toward first light.

You will see only trees, then us
waiting, faces shadowed, mother's
breath like wind. Walls move.
I will drop doorkeys. We're yours,

singing in the dawn. We're those
who rub their eyes and grin when
steam breaks at the stationhouse
and all creation steps down safe.